Orange Line 3

Workbook

Herausgeber: Dr. Frank Haß

Ernst Klett Verlag
Stuttgart • Leipzig

Unit 1

England now and then

10/2

1 What happened first? Put the pictures in the right order.

10/2

2 Complete the sentences.

Normans | Industrial Revolution | fought against the English | Stonehenge ✓ | border | other northern countries | 4,000 years | Vikings | build Hadrian's Wall

1. Stonehenge __________ is an old circle of stones. It is __________ old.
2. The Romans took six years to __________ in the north of England. They started to build this __________ in the year 122.
3. The __________ invaded York in 866. They came from Denmark, Norway and __________ .
4. The __________ came from France. In 1066 they __________ near Hastings and won.
5. The __________ happened in cities like Manchester.

11/3

3 (WRITING) Write a fact card about Stonehenge.

Stonehenge

12/2

1 Complete the crossword.

1. My brother is i__________ in football.
2. A__________ everyone I know can speak English.
3. You have to cross the r__________ .
4. That Viking h__________ is a brilliant souvenir!
5. The best shops are in the city c__________ .
6. That shop doesn't s__________ souvenirs.

Can you find the secret word? __________

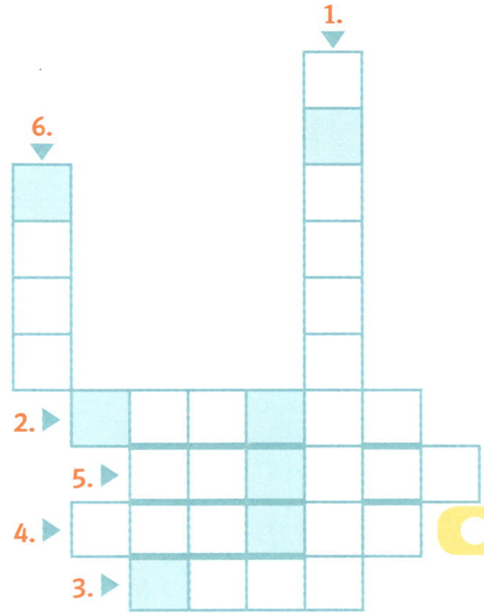

2 Shops and things you can buy there

3/4a)

a) Write the names of the shops and then more things you can buy there.

1.

1. It's a baker's.__________ You can buy: __________
2. __________ You can buy: __________

2.

3.

3. __________ You can buy: __________
4. __________ You can buy: __________

4.

5.

5. __________ You can buy: __________
6. __________ You can buy: __________

6.

3/4b)

b) Write the names of the shops and complete the sentences.

1. You can buy jewellery__________ at __________ . 
2. At a __________ you can buy __________ . 
3. You can buy __________ . 
4. At a __________ . 
5. You __________ . 

3 (LISTENING) Listen to the dialogue and tick the right box.

1
13/5

	right	wrong
1. The woman wants to buy a bird.	☐	☐
2. The dog snacks are on the shelves with the dog food.	☐	☐
3. The dog snacks look like sausages.	☐	☐
4. The blue collar has a cat on it.	☐	☐
5. The fish food is on the right.	☐	☐

14/8a)

4 Complete the sentences. Use the simple present.

1. Sam _doesn't know_ his way around York. (not know)
2. He __________ to buy some souvenirs for his family. (want)
3. His sister __________ magazines, so he goes to a newsagent's. (like)
4. His parents __________ lots of sport, so he goes to a sports shop. (play)
5. He __________ much time, so he asks the way. (not have)
6. Mrs Jenkins says, "I usually __________ to the shops on the Shambles." (go)
7. "The other shops __________ very good souvenirs." (not sell)
8. Mrs Jenkins __________ Sam the best bargains. (show)

14/8a)

5 Put in the right forms of the simple present.

ask	be ✓	come	buy	have
not want	rain	not have	be	

Our shop _is_ on the Shambles, a beautiful street. Tourists __________ from many different countries to see it! Our shop __________ a lot of souvenirs and __________ always busy. People often __________ our funny presents like Viking helmets and joke books. And, of course, we sell a lot of umbrellas because it often __________ in York. People __________ to get wet! People often __________ if we sell snacks or drinks, but our shop __________ any because there are lots of other shops for that.

14/8b)

6 Make sentences.

Work with a partner. Make cards with these words. You can add more cards with your own words. Make sentences with the words on the cards.

I	don't	like	football	often
Anna	doesn't	play	TV	always
we		eat	chocolate	never
you		…	…	…
they				
…				

Example:

I	often	play	football

14/9

7 Sam talks to a girl at the Viking Centre. Write his questions and the girl's answers.

Sam:	Girl:
1. live in York?	☺
2. like the museum?	☺
3. often come to the museum?	☹
4. know a lot about York?	☺
5. like the Vikings?	☺
6. have a Viking helmet?	☹
7. know a good café near here?	☺
8. want to go to the café with me?	☹

1. Do you live in York? – Yes, I do.
2. ______
3. ______
4. ______
5. ______
6. ______
7. ______
8. ______

/10a)

8 Now Sam talks to a tour guide. Read the guide's answers and write Sam's questions.

1. (When • the tour • start)
   When does the tour start ?
   The tour starts in ten minutes.
2. (How much • be • it)
   How much ______ ?
   It's five pounds.
3. (Where • it • stop) ______ ?
   It stops at the Viking Centre.
4. (How old • be • buildings • on this road) ______ ?
   The buildings on this road are 300 years old.
5. (What • be • your favourite place in York) ______ ?
   The river is my favourite place.
6. (How often • you • work) ______ ?
   I work every Tuesday and Saturday.
7. (Where • be • nearest toilet) ______ ?
   The nearest toilet is next to the church.

9 Your favourite place in your town

15/10b)

Ask your partner about his / her favourite place in his / her town. Write three questions.
Ask your partner these questions and write down his / her answers in your exercise book.

1. ______________________________
2. ______________________________
3. ______________________________

10 Directions

15/11

a) Collect phrases you need to give directions.

1. ____________ 2. ____________ 3. ____________ 4. ____________

5. ____________ 6. ____________ 7. ____________ 8. ____________

b) You are at ✕ on the map. Write directions.

1. to the baker's:

Go straight on.

____

____

2. to the post office:

____

____

____

____

3. to the book shop:

____

____

____

c) Choose a different place to go to and write the directions in your exercise book.

d) Let your partner guess where you want to go.

16/1

1 Write the words under the pictures.

1. ________________

2. ________________

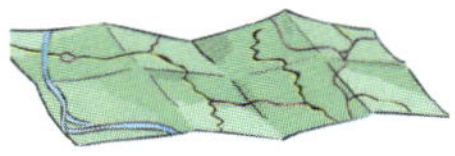

3. ________________

4. ________________

5. ________________

6. ________________

7. ________________

8. ________________

9. ________________

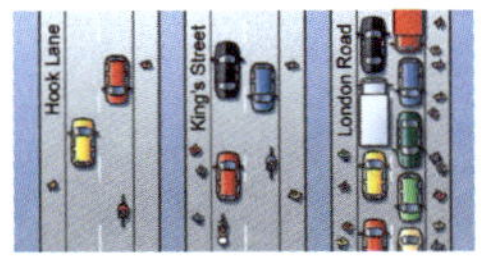

10. ________________

7/3a)

2 Underline the right word.

1. 100 years ago there was a lot of industry • information • invitation.
2. You can milk a cabbage • cow • chair.
3. Manchester has a lot of inhabitants • islands • ideas.
4. You can live in the carpet • clock • city centre.
5. Something bad is unfair • unhappy • upset.
6. You can walk in the moments • menus • mountains.

7/3b)

3 Complete the sentences.

1. A very small thing is tiny ________________ .
2. A village which is at the seaside is on the ________________ .
3. I usually get around by bus or train. I use ________________ .
4. A very big thing is ________________ .
5. Poland is hundreds of miles away. That's a long ________________ .
6. Britain is an island. The sea is to ________________ .

17/4
2

4 (LISTENING) Listen to Oliver talking about Bristol.

a) Put a circle around the right answer.

1. Bristol is in the north • south • east • west of England.
2. There are about 1 million • 500,000 • 5000 inhabitants.
3. Oliver doesn't like the country • the city centre • the train.
4. At weekends Oliver goes to concerts • listens to music • rides his bike .
5. People in the past went from Bristol to America by car • ship • plane.

b) Listen again and write notes. Use your notes to write a fact card for Bristol in your exercise book.

5 Write about Tom's week. Use the simple past.

18/6

a) Put in the right words.

work	help	play ✓	watch	talk	call
clean	not watch	stay	not milk	not do	be

On Monday afternoon Tom played __________ cricket after school and his dad __________ on the farm. Tom __________ his homework because he came home very late. The next day Tom's mum __________ his dad on the farm. They milked the cows, but they __________ their goats, Bert and Daisy. Bert and Daisy __________ happy about that. On Wednesday Tom __________ TV with his friends. They __________ Tom's favourite programme because his friends wanted to watch a film about a fire in a big city. On Thursday evening Tom __________ his friend Mike. They __________ about their new teacher. After school on Friday Tom __________ his dad's car. On Friday evening everybody __________ at home.

b) What did Tom's family do on Saturday? Look at the picture and write sentences.

1. Tom __________
2. His dad __________
3. His mum __________
4. The cat __________

6 Put in the right forms.

18/6

infinitive	simple past	infinitive	simple past
take		go	
	drove		saw
	fought	win	
have		swim	
	met		did
buy		write	

Eine Liste der unregelmäßigen Verben findest du in deinem Buch auf Seite 219–220.

7 Hannah's Saturday

take | not buy | meet
spend | get | go ✓
not understand | leave | do

a) Put in the right simple past forms.

3/7a)

Last Saturday I *went* into Manchester city centre with some friends. I __________ my friend Maxine outside our favourite clothes shop. We __________ about an hour trying on some clothes, but I __________ anything. Maxine __________ a really cool T-shirt. We __________ the city centre at about 3 p.m. and __________ the bus to my flat. Then we __________ our Maths homework together because it's easier when you do it with a friend. I __________ some things and Maths is Maxine's best subject.

b) What did / didn't you do last weekend? Write five sentences in your exercise book.

3/7b)

8 Look at the pictures. Write questions and answers.

19/8

go

take

swim

eat

buy

1. Did Tom go *to the city centre? – No, he didn't.*
2. Did __________
3. __________
4. __________
5. __________

9 Ask your partner.

19/8

Ask your partner about his / her last holidays. Write four questions.
Ask your partner your questions and write down his / her answers in your exercise book.

1. *Where did you* __________
2. *What did* __________
3. *When* __________
4. __________

10 Put in the right simple past forms.

19/8

Tom: Hi Hannah! What did you do (do) at the weekend?

Hannah: I __________ (go) to the Manchester Museum.

Tom: I ______________ (not / know) that Manchester had a museum. What can you see there?

Hannah: It's about Manchester's history. Manchester ____________ (become) a big city in the Industrial Revolution.

Tom: When ________ (be) the Industrial Revolution? I'm no good at history!

Hannah: It ________ (be) about 200 years ago. Many factories ____________ (open) and people __________ (go) to the city to work in them.

Tom: What ________________ (see) in the museum?

Hannah: There are lots of pictures of old Manchester and stories about people who ________ (live) then. Life wasn't easy for them. The city ________ (be) dirty and the houses ________ (be) small.

Tom: How long ______________ (be) in the museum?

Hannah: About two hours. I ____________ (learn) a lot. You should go there too!

11 (WRITING) Write a text about Newcastle.

19/9

a) Read the fact card about Newcastle.

Newcastle

City in northeast England,
near the border to Scotland.
Not far from the sea.

In the past: Romans, Industrial Revolution, factories

Today: Big city (1.5 million), famous football club (Newcastle United)

What to do? Big parks, near the beach

b) Write a text about Newcastle.

____

____

____

____

____

____

____

____

____

____

____

____

____

19/9

1 (SOUNDS) Tongue twisters

a) Say the tongue twisters loud. Say each sentence again and again and speak faster each time.

She has her socks in her shoes.
The salt is on the shelf in the shop.
That shop sends snacks to the seaside.
Do you like this scarf or this T-shirt?

3 b) Now listen to the tongue twisters. Did you say all the words right? Try again.

19/9

2 (SPEAKING) Give directions.

a) Work with a partner and make a dialogue.
Use the map on the right.

post office | sports shop | park | card shop | burger bar | baker's | toilet | shoe shop | supermarket | souvenir shop

Is it far away? | Can I walk there? | It doesn't take long. | You're welcome.

turn right | turn left | walk past | go straight on | cross the road | walk down

Partner A

Excuse me, please. Is there a ______________ near here?

Partner B

Yes, there is. ______________
____
____

Partner A

Thank you. ______________

Partner B

No, it isn't. ______________ .

Partner A

OK, that's great. ______________ .

Partner B

______________ .

b) Act your dialogue.

c) Make two more dialogues and act them with your partner.

23/7

1 (READING) Read the text.

A modern miner

Today there are no coal mines left[1] in England. Hatfield Mine in Doncaster, North England was the last mine and it closed in 2015. John Barrow worked there for over 20 years. Here he tells us about his work in the mines.

“Work in the mines changed a lot over the last 100 years. I started to work there when I was 16, but I first went down into the mine when I was 18. For the first month an older miner took me with him. He looked after me and taught me how to stay safe. Like 100 years ago, the miners were all very good friends: everyone looked after the new miners.

The work in a mine is a difficult job, but it was much harder 100 years ago. Then, they had to push and pull the heavy coal. When I worked there, machines did all the hard work. I worked the machines with a remote control[2], a bit like a TV remote. We had lamps in all the tunnels, so we didn’t have to work in the dark any more.

It was still a dangerous job because there were sometimes accidents or gas explosions. About 30 years ago we used canaries to warn us about gas. We talked to the canaries – they were like our pets. Later there was an alarm[3] if there was gas in the mine. When I worked there, I heard the alarm over 20 times, but luckily there was never an explosion.

My grandfather and father were also miners. When I was a little boy, almost everyone in my village worked at the mine. But now the mine has closed. Coal isn’t popular today. This makes me sad because it is the end of a part of English history. But it’s also good news because the future will be better. We can use sunshine[4] and wind today, so coal isn’t so important these days.”

1 left [left] – *übrig;* 2 remote control [rɪˌməʊt kənˈtrəʊl] – *Fernbedienung;* 3 alarm [əˈlɑːm] – *Alarm;* 4 sunshine [ˈsʌnʃaɪn] – *Sonnenschein*

2 Tick the right box.

23/7

1. What happened when John was 16?
   a) He went down into the mine. ☐
   b) He started working at the mine. ☐
   c) He got a canary. ☐

2. 100 years ago mining was ...
   a) boring. ☐
   b) more exciting. ☐
   c) harder. ☐

3. What happened if there was gas in the mine?
   a) There was an alarm. ☐
   b) There was a fire. ☐
   c) They closed the mine. ☐

4. John's grandfather and father ...
   a) were popular. ☐
   b) were miners. ☐
   c) talked to the canaries. ☐

5. Hatfield Mine was ...
   a) the last mine in England. ☐
   b) the most important mine in England. ☐
   c) the most dangerous mine in England. ☐

6. John is sad because ...
   a) it is the end of a part of English history. ☐
   b) he liked his job. ☐
   c) his dad was a miner. ☐

3 Answer the questions.

23/7

Achte auf die Zeiten!

1. Why did John go down the mine with an older miner?

   ____

2. Why was the job easier for John than for the miners 100 years ago?

   ____

3. Why was it still a dangerous job?

   ____

4. Why isn't coal popular anymore?

   ____

4 (WRITING) Mines in Germany

23/7

Find out about mines in Germany. Use the internet for help and write a short text about one.

____

____

____

____

____

____

____

INTERNET

WOMEN'S FOOTBALL

Women have played football for longer than you might think. The world's first women's football team was called 'The British Ladies'. It started in 1894 in England, but the women could not play on football fields. Instead, they had to play on rugby fields. This changed about 50 years ago and now women's football is one of the world's fastest growing sports.

Today most countries in the world have women's football teams and there are several important competitions, for example the European Women's Competition and the World Cup. Although women's football is more popular today, you can't watch a lot of matches on TV because a lot of people still think men's football is more interesting. It is also more difficult for women's teams to find good sponsors.

Wenn du einen englischen Text liest, musst du nicht jedes Wort verstehen. Lies dir die Frage genau durch und suche die Wörter im Text, nach denen gefragt wird.

24/1

1 (MEDIATION) Beantworte die Fragen.

1. In welchem Land gab es das erste Frauenfußballteam? ______
2. Seit wann wird Frauenfußball immer beliebter? ______
3. Warum werden im Fernsehen nicht so viele Spiele gezeigt?

______

24/1

2 (MEDIATION) At a football match

Markiere dir zuerst, welche Sätze auf Deutsch und welche Sätze auf Englisch sein müssen.

Du schaust dir in England ein Fußballspiel im Stadion an. Der deutsche Mann neben dir möchte sich mit einer anderen Zuschauerin auf Englisch unterhalten. Hilf ihm dabei.

Man: Kannst du sie fragen, wie alt der Fußballclub ist?

You: ______

Woman: It's over 100 years old.

You: ______

Man: Wie viele Spiele haben sie dieses Jahr schon gewonnen?

You: ______

Woman: They've only won five matches. But I hope they win today!

You: ______

Man: Sag ihr, dass sie heute aber nicht gut spielen.

You: ______

Woman: That's right! They can play better than this.

You: ______

1. Löse alle Aufgaben.
2. Überprüfe deine Lösungen online. Gib dazu den 🌐-Code (nach Ziel 5) auf www.klett.de ein.
3. Gib dir selbst Punkte. Wenn du weniger als die Hälfte der Punkte hast, male das Kästchen rot aus und übe auf den Step by step-Seiten (z. B. bei Unit 1 auf S. 18–19).

Ziel 1: I can understand information about historical places in England.

→ ⦾ 5hu92e

4000 years ago, a stone circle was built in the south of England. We don't know who built it or why it was built. This mystery makes it so interesting that more than a million tourists visit Stonehenge every year.

Different people invaded England in the past. The Romans came first and built Hadrian's Wall in the north of England. The Vikings invaded the English city of York in 866. In 1066 the Normans came across the sea from France and a Norman became the new king of England.

The Industrial Revolution was from 1780–1840. There were lots of factories and the cities were often dirty. Today there is less industry and the cities are much nicer.

Answer the questions.

1. Who built Stonehenge and why? ______________________

____

2. Why do so many tourists visit Stonehenge every year? ______________________
3. Who invaded England in the past? ______________________

____

4. Where did the Normans come from? ______________________
5. What were the cities like in the Industrial Revolution? ______________________

____

____ 5P

p. 18/1

Ziel 2: I can give and understand directions.

→ ⦾ 5z8br5 → ⦾ iy5v47

a) You are at ✕ on the map. Read the directions. Where do they take you?

Go straight on. Walk past the post office. Turn right and walk past the park. Turn right and it's on the left.

____

b) Write directions to the sports shop:

____

____

____

____ 6P

p. 18/2

Ziel 3: I can talk in more detail about where I live.

→ ◎ bu465i → ◎ eb9a6m

a) Collect words and phrases you can use to describe a town, city or village

Where is it?	What is it?	How many inhabitants?

What is it like? What can you see there?	What can you do there?	My favourite place

b) Write a short text about where you live.

___

___

___

___

___

7P

→ p. 19/3

Ziel 4: I can understand a story from the past.

→ ◎ zu2x3g

Read the text on pages 20–22 in your book again. Tick the right box.

	right	wrong
1. Jonas opens the door when the coal arrives.	☐	☐
2. When the canary sings, there is gas in the mine.	☐	☐
3. Jonas stopped talking because he was sick.	☐	☐
4. One day the canary stopped singing.	☐	☐
5. Suddenly Jonas shouted, "Gas!"	☐	☐
6. The canary died in the explosion.	☐	☐
7. Everyone said thank you.	☐	☐

7P

→ p. 19/4

Ziel 5: I can pass on information about the history of a sport.

Cricket

Football is the most-watched sport in the world, but did you know that cricket is the second most popular sport?

Cricket is very old: children played it in Norman times. The adult game began about 400 years ago. In 1800 only rich men played cricket. It was a good sport for old and young men because it was quite easy and slow. It was so slow that a match took five days! It was normal to have lunch or tea while the game was played. It is still normal today for cricket players to have lunch and snacks together when they are not playing.

Cricket also became popular in countries like Australia, India, Pakistan and Sri Lanka. Today there are famous competitions between these countries. The most famous is called 'The Ashes', which is played between Australia and England every year in July. It is played in the country which won the year before. The cup that the winners get is probably the smallest prize in the world! Australia has won The Ashes more often than England.

a) Beantworte die Fragen.

1. Warum ist Cricket ein guter Sport für Jung und Alt? ______
2. Was kann man machen, wenn ein Spiel lange dauert? ______
3. Wie heißt der berühmteste Cricket-Wettbewerb und was können die Mannschaften gewinnen?

______

b) Du bist mit deiner Familie bei einem Fußballspiel. Ein junger Mann aus England will sich mit deinem Vater unterhalten. Vermittle zwischen den beiden.

Man: Hi! It's a great match, isn't it? Do you watch every match here?

You: ______

______

Your dad: Sag ihm, dass wir jeden Samstag hierher kommen. Frag ihn, ob er auch Fußball spielt.

You: ______

Man: Yes, I play football for the club in my town. Do you play football too?

You: ______

______

Your dad: Sag ihm, dass ich in der Vergangenheit gespielt habe und dass du jedes Wochenende spielst.

You: ______

7P

→p. 19/5

○ **Ziel 1: I can understand infomation about historical places in England.**

4000 years ago, Stonehenge was built in the south of England. We don't know who built it or why. More than a million tourists visit Stonehenge every year.

The Romans built Hadrian's Wall in the north of England. The Vikings invaded the English city of York in 866. In 1066 the Normans came across the sea from France.

The Industrial Revolution was from 1780–1840. Lots of factories were built.

Right or wrong? Tick the right box.

	right	wrong
1. Stonehenge was built 4,000 years ago.	☐	☐
2. 100,000 tourists visit Stonehenge every year.	☐	☐
3. The Romans built Hadrian's Wall.	☐	☐
4. The Vikings invaded York.	☐	☐
5. The Normans came from Norway.	☐	☐
6. In the Industrial Revolution lots of factories were built.	☐	☐

○ **Ziel 2: I can give and understand directions.**

You are at ✕ on the map.
Where do the directions take you?

1. Go straight on. It's opposite the post office.

   ____

2. Go straight on and take the first street on the right. Walk past the park. Cross the street. Walk past the clothes shop and it's on your left.

   ____

3. Go straight on and take the first street on the left. Cross the street.

   ____

4. Go straight on. Walk past the park. Cross the street and it's on the right.

   ____

○ **Ziel 3: I can talk in more detail about where I live.**

Fill in the gaps with words about your town or city.

I live in ______________ . It is a __________ (big / small) __________ (city / town / village) in the ______________ (north / south / east / west) of Germany. ______________ is ______________ (close to / far from) ______________ . There are ______________ (cinemas / parks / cafés / shops). My favourite place is ______________ because ______________ .

○ **Ziel 4: I can understand a story from the past.**

Read the text on pages 20–22 in your book again. Complete the sentences.

stopped talking | there was gas in the mine | the canary with them | the canary was still alive | he shouted, "GAS!" | when the coal arrives

1. Jonas works in a mine and opens a door ______________ .
2. When Jonas' brother died, Jonas ______________ .
3. One day the canary in the mine stopped singing. Jonas knew ______________ .
4. Jonas wanted to warn the other miners. Suddenly, ______________ .
5. Everyone ran out of the mine and they took ______________ .
6. Nobody was hurt and ______________ .

○ **Ziel 5: I can pass on information about the history of a sport.**

Lies den Text und beantworte die Fragen.

When people started to play tennis, the balls were made of wool, or even hair! Today all tennis balls are rubber.

In the past tennis balls were also a different colour, usually black or white. The ball became yellow in 1972 so that people could see it on colour TV.

Although it is small, the ball is very important! Players often take four or five and choose the best one.

1. Woraus hat man früher Tennisbälle gemacht?

____

2. Warum sind Tennisbälle heute gelb?

____

____

3. Warum haben Tennisspieler oft mehrere Bälle?

____

____

Boy from York finds Roman treasure

A 14-year-old boy called Luke Stanton has found Roman coins!

Luke wanted a new hobby. His father asked him if he wanted to look for treasure with a metal detector[1]. “I laughed at him because I thought it would be boring. I said I would try it for a day.” Luke and his father went to a field on their farm, in Kellington, Yorkshire.

After only 20 minutes with the metal detector, it made a sound. Luke made a hole and soon he found a big wooden[2] box.
“I knew it was old. The wood was black and there were holes in it. I got excited!”

There were a lot of old coins in the box, but Luke didn’t think they were special.
“All the coins were green and stuck together. I called Dad and when he saw them, he knew they were special. He told me to stop and called the museum in York .”

After the museum workers arrived, they carefully took the coins back to the museum. They cleaned them very slowly and saw that they were Roman coins. “They called us, and told us that they were real Roman coins. We couldn’t believe it!” says Luke. “They also told us you should never dig[3] on your own. If you find something very old, you can damage[4] it.”

The coins are about 2,300 years old. At that time Romans lived in Yorkshire, which is not very far from Hadrian’s Wall.
The museum workers told Luke why somebody would leave the coins in a field.
“At that time lots of people stole[5] money. Somebody probably left the money there because it was a safe place, but then something happened to them and they never came back for it.”

“I love my new hobby!” says Luke. “It’s not boring at all! I’m not sure if I’ll ever find anything so exciting again, but I’ll try.”

1 metal detector ['metl dɪˌtektə] – *Metalldetektor;* 2 wooden ['wʊdn] – *aus Holz;* 3 dig, dug, dug [dɪg] – *graben;* 4 damage ['dæmɪdʒ] – *beschädigen;* 5 steal, stole, stolen [sti:l] – *stehlen*

31/2 ↗ ## 1 Skim the text.

1. What kind of text is it? ______________________________
2. What does the title tell you about the story? ______________________________

31/2 ↗ ## 2 Scan the text.

Key words can help you to understand the text. You can find the key words when you ask the questions Who? What? Where? When? Why? Underline the key words in the text. Then fill in the table.

Who?	
What?	
Where?	
When?	
Why?	

31/2 ↗ ## 3 Write a summary.

Use the key words from exercise 2 and write a summary of the text.

Luke Stanton lives on a farm in Kellington in Yorkshire.
One day he wants a new hobby. His father ______________________________

____

____

____

____

____

____

____

____

____

____

Wenn du einen Text zusammenfasst, benutzt du normalerweise das simple present. Benutze das simple past nur, wenn du über vergangene Ereignisse schreibst.

Unit 2

Adventures in Wales

32/2 **1 Look at the pictures.**

a) Write a title for each picture.

1. The highest ______________________ 2. ______________________

3. ______________________ 4. ______________________

b) Choose one of the pictures and write a short text about it.

____

____

____

c) Read your text to a partner. Can he / she guess which picture it is?

2 (LISTENING) Listen to the interview and tick the right box.

4
33/3

	right	wrong
1. Cardiff is called Europe's oldest capital.	☐	☐
2. If you like history, you can visit the museum in Cardiff.	☐	☐
3. There are no old buildings in Cardiff.	☐	☐
4. The Wales Millennium Centre has a theatre and a cinema.	☐	☐
5. Cardiff has lots of good restaurants.	☐	☐
6. You can have a Welsh cake in a café.	☐	☐

1 Write the activities under the pictures.

34/2

 1. ____________

 2. ____________

 3. ____________

 4. ____________

 5. ____________

 6. ____________

 7. ____________

 8. ____________

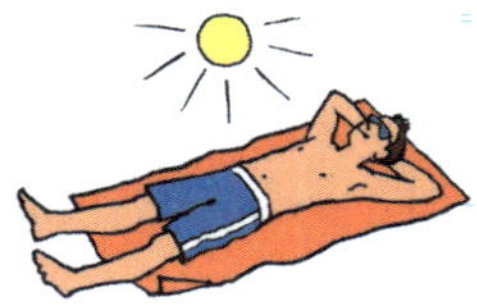 9. ____________

 10. ____________

2 Put in the right word.

34/3

myself · yourself · himself · herself · itself · ourselves · themselves

1. We enjoyed *ourselves* ____________ at the party.
2. Did you do your homework ____________ ?
3. Do you want to try this cake? I made it ____________ .
4. She cut ____________ with a knife.
5. He hurt ____________ when he fell off his bike.
6. This computer programme can start ____________ .
7. They saw ____________ on the photo.

3 Word search

35/5a)

a) Find 16 words and write them down.

instructor	*a*
u	*s*
i	*c*
e	*r*
m	*e*
q	*t*
d	*w*
r	*o*

A	G	C	E	I	F	G	N	G	Q	U	I	T	E
N	D	H	E	N	M	Y	S	E	L	F	S	V	H
Y	G	E	R	S	H	R	J	I	E	Z	E	Z	F
W	E	E	R	T	S	U	E	N	U	V	V	D	F
A	Q	K	K	R	W	L	N	D	S	B	J	A	E
Y	U	Y	K	U	E	E	O	O	E	G	U	N	F
E	I	D	G	C	U	E	U	O	F	G	F	G	J
S	P	G	M	T	J	K	G	R	U	Q	W	E	O
H	M	J	E	O	R	U	H	B	L	U	R	R	U
O	E	S	H	R	J	R	F	J	E	P	U	O	T
U	N	U	H	J	G	T	I	M	E	T	R	U	D
L	T	W	O	O	D	R	J	Y	Y	E	U	S	O
D	G	R	E	L	A	X	I	N	G	U	E	U	O
F	G	J	T	T	T	A	Z	J	N	G	K	D	R

b) Choose four words. Write a sentence for each word in your exercise book.

35/5b)

4 (WRITING) Use the words to write sentences about people you know.

competitive | patient | successful | clever

1. My friend ______ is ______ because ______
2. ______
3. ______
4. ______

36/8a)

5 Adjective or Adverb?

a) Put a circle around the right letter.

	adjective	adverb
1. nice	(L)	M
2. easy	O	E
3. carefully	S	U

	adjective	adverb
4. happily	A	D
5. dangerous	L	T
6. excitingly	E	Y

b) Make an adverb with the letters in the circles: ______

6 Write sentences with adverbs.

36/8a)

a) Complete the sentences.

1. I ran quickly ______ to catch the ball. (quick)
2. The people watched the tennis match ______ . (quiet)
3. We won the match ______ . (easy)
4. We went ______ down the river in our boats. (careful)
5. She danced ______ around the house. (happy)
6. When our team won, we shouted ______ . (loud)
7. I climbed ______ down the mountain. (safe)
8. They swam ______ back to the beach. (slow)

36/8b)

b) Write sentences with adverbs.

ride bike ✓ | play football | swim | play tennis | sing | eat

1. I ride my bike carefully.
2. ______
3. ______
4. ______
5. ______
6. ______

7 Adjective or adverb? Put a circle around the right form.

36/9

1. That football player is really good • well.
2. I think tennis is a slow • slowly game.
3. He surfs quite bad • badly.
4. Rock climbing can be a very dangerous • dangerously activity.
5. To play rugby, you must be strong and learn quick • quickly.
6. The instructor was very angry • angrily with the team.
7. She rode the horse nervous • nervously.
8. The crowd watched the match excited • excitedly.

8 Complete the table.

36/9

adjective	adverb
bad	badly
heavy	
good	
	fast
	cleverly
careful	
	nicely
happy	
hard	

Sei vorsichtig bei Wörtern wie *careful* und *easy*!
carefully
easily

9 Adjective or adverb? Put in the right forms.

36/9

sunny | good | great | nice | careful | clear | slow

At the weekend I went rock climbing in Wales. It was really *great* ______ and I wasn't scared. The mountain was quite high, so I climbed ______ and ______. The instructor told us very ______ what we had to do. I learned a lot about how to climb ______. I had a really ______ day, and the weather was ______ too!

❀ 10 (WRITING) My best friend

37/10a) **a)** Make a mind map about your best friend. Use adverbs and / or adjectives.

what he / she looks like:

where he / she lives:

my best friend

his / her hobbies:

what he / she is like:

37/10b) **b)** Use your mind map and write a short text about your best friend.

You can put a picture here.

❀ 11 (SPEAKING) My favourite activity

36/11 **a)** Tell your partner about your favourite activity.

My favourite activity is …
I like it because …
You must be …
You need …

b) Ask your partner questions about his / her favourite activity.

39/5

1 What are the body parts?

39/5

2 Match the sentences.

1. I've cut my foot.
2. I've broken my leg.
3. I have a headache.
4. I've twisted my ankle.
5. I've burnt my hand.
6. I've got a sore throat.

Drink some warm tea.
You need a bandage.
Cool it with water.
Put a plaster on it.
Take a tablet.
You need a cast.

3 (WRITING) Look at the picture and write the text messages.

/6a) a) What happened to Tim? Write Tim's text message to his mum.

/6b) b) Write his mum's answer message.

5
39/6

4 (LISTENING) Listen to the emergeny call.

a) Answer the questions.

1. What is the caller's name? ______
2. What service does she need? ______
3. What has happened? ______
4. What must Laura do? ______

b) What is Laura's phone number? ______

40/7

5 What has happened? Look at the picture and complete the sentences.

1. There has been an accident.
2. The boy ______________ his bike.
3. The boy ______________ his leg.
4. Two policemen ______________ .
5. An ambulance ______________ .
6. The doctor ______________ a bandage on the boy's leg.
7. The dogs ______________ the sausages.
8. The women ______________ the shop.

leave | put | fall off | come | hurt | be ✓ | take | arrive

40/7

6 Complete the table.

infinitive	simple past	past participle
be	was / were	
	came	
do		
	felt	
find		
	forgot	
	got	
go		
		known
	made	
put		

7 What have they already done? What haven't they done yet?

/8a) a) Look at the pictures and write sentences.

finish homework

tidy room

make dinner

1. She has already finished her homework.
2. He ______
3. He ______

catch bird

buy bananas

eat food

4. They ______
5. She ______
6. The dog ______

/8b) b) What haven't you done yet? Write three sentences.

______

______

______

40/8

8 Ask your partner.

a) Write questions for your partner.

1. have an accident? Have you ever had an accident? Yes, I have.
2. be in an ambulance? ______
3. break your arm or leg? ______
4. need a cast? ______
5. call the police? ______
6. have stomach ache? ______

b) Your partner answers your questions and writes his / her answers in your workbook.

c) Use the words below and write three more questions and write down your partner's answers.

injection operation medicine day off cuddly toy

9 Complete the sentences. Use the simple past or present perfect.

41/9a)

a) Underline the signal words in the sentences.

b) Complete the sentences with the simple past or present perfect.

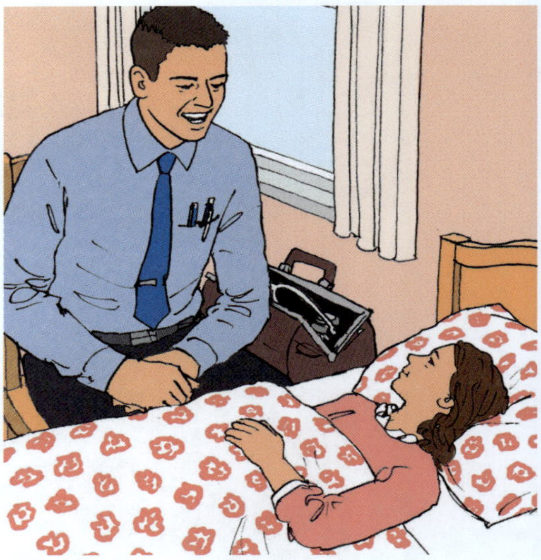

1. My sister ____________ fish and chips yesterday. (eat)
2. She ____________ stomach ache last night. (have)
3. The doctor ____________ already ________________ at our house. (arrive)
4. We ______________________ her any tablets yet. (not give)
5. The doctor __________ already ______________ to her. (talk)
6. I _____________ never ____________ stomach ache. (have)
7. But I ____________ very ill last year. (be)

10 Complete the dialogue with the simple past or present perfect.

41/9a)

Elena: Hi Flynn! How are you?

Flynn: OK, but I ____________ a little accident yesterday. (have)

Elena: Oh no! What happened?

Flynn: I ____________ over during football last night. (fall)

Elena: Are you OK?

Flynn: Yes, but I __________________________ my ankle. (sprain)

Elena: Really? _____________ you _____________ to the doctor yet? (be)

Flynn: Yes, I _____________ already _____________ (see) a doctor.
He ____________ a bandage on it this morning and _____________ me some tablets. (put, give)

Elena: Well, I hope it feels better soon!

11 (WRITING) Interview your partner about an emergency.

41/9b)

a) Write some questions for your partner.

____

____

____

____

____

- Have you ever been / had ...
- When... / Where...?
- What...?
- Who...?
- Was it scary / exciting / ...?

b) Act the interview with your partner.

1 (SPEAKING) Make an emergency call.

1/10

a) Complete the dialogue.

Operator

Hello, ____________________ services.
How can I help you?

What has happened?

OK, where are you?

And what is your name and phone number?

I'm sending an ___________ now.

Caller

Help! I need ________________________ !

A man ____________________ .
He has hurt __________________ .

I'm in ______________________________ .

My name is ______________ and my phone number is ___________________________ .

Thank you.

b) Act the dialogue with your partner.

2 (SPEAKING) Make an emergency call.

1/10

a) Choose one of the pictures and do a role play with your partner.

b) Act your role play for the class.

c) The ambulance has arrived. The doctor talks to a person who is hurt. Make a dialogue.

43/4

1 (READING) Read the report.

Our trip to Cardiff

(by Melanie Gould) Year 9 had an exciting trip to Cardiff on Wednesday afternoon. First, we went to Cardiff Castle. The guide, Louise, told us lots about its history and some cool things about the ghosts there. Then we went to Bute Park next to the castle and ate our packed lunch. We also played football for a while and listened to some music. The weather was really nice and sunny.

After lunch we went on a visit to the Millennium Stadium. It is a really big sports stadium in the centre of Cardiff. There are lots of big sports matches there and music concerts too. Our guide used to be a rugby player and played rugby in the stadium in 2012. I told her I preferred football. ☺

We visited the rooms where the players get dressed before a match and the room where all the reporters from the newspapers watch the matches. We then saw the room where they keep all the big sports prizes. After that, we visited the 'President's Box', which is where the Royal Family sit if they visit the stadium. I sat in the same chair as Prince Harry! We then went down the long tunnel where the players walk into the stadium when there is a match. It was pretty cool!

Then the visit was over, but we couldn't find James, Bas or Daniel. Ms Field was really angry (and a bit worried I think). Louise used her phone to call around the stadium to try to find them. Suddenly someone saw them. Laura and Ms Field went to get them and we all went with them. The boys were on the grass! The caretaker of the stadium was so angry. ☹ He shouted, "Get off the grass! You will ruin it! It's wet!". Then James fell over and was holding his leg. The caretaker went and got the boys off the grass. Ms Field was not happy. James said, "I think I have twisted my ankle." The boys were in big trouble!

We said bye to Louise and then came the best part of the day. We all went shopping for an hour. Well, not everyone. James, Bas and Daniel had to go and sit on the bus with Ms Field and do write about the trip to Cardiff! Ms Field put a bandage on James' ankle.

I found a cute little clothes shop and bought a new skirt and a scarf. Then we all went to the sweet shop and bought some sweets for the trip back to school.

Our trip to Cardiff was really fun and I loved the Millennium Stadium and the shops in Cardiff.

43/4

2 Right, wrong or not in the text? Tick the right box.

	right	wrong	not in the text
1. The class went to Cardiff Castle.	☐	☐	☐
2. They had lunch in a restaurant.	☐	☐	☐
3. The Millennium Stadium opened in 1999.	☐	☐	☐
4. Their guide used to be a rugby player.	☐	☐	☐
5. They visited the rooms where the players get dressed.	☐	☐	☐
6. Five boys from the class went on the grass.	☐	☐	☐
7. One of the boys hurt his leg.	☐	☐	☐
8. Ms Field called an ambulance.	☐	☐	☐

43/4

3 Read the report again.

a) Find the answers to the questions below in the text and underline them.

b) Write the answers to the questions.

1. What sights did the class visit in Cardiff?

____

2. Which rooms did they see in the Millennium Stadium?

____

____

3. What did James, Bas and Daniel do?

____

4. What happened to James?

____

5. What did James, Bas and Daniel do while the others went shopping?

____

6. What did Mel like best in Cardiff?

____

43/4

4 (WRITING) Make a leaflet for the Millennium Stadium.

a) Collect information from the text about the stadium.

b) Find more information and some photos on the internet.

c) Make your leaflet.

d) Present your leaflet to the class.

Learn to surf in Wales!

Come to the beautiful beaches of West Wales to learn this cool water sport.
All our friendly instructors have surfed for many years.
They will show you the equipment, teach you how to catch a wave, how to surf it and most importantly, how to keep safe in the water.
We have classes from Monday to Saturday in the morning, afternoon and evening on some of the most spectacular beaches in Great Britain.
To take part in our classes you don't need to have surfed before but you need to be a good swimmer and over 12 years old.

For prices, dates and more information, look on our website or call 07756 7453884

1 (MEDIATION) Beanworte die Fragen.

44/1

Du machst demnächst mit deiner Familie Urlaub in Wales und willst dort surfen lernen.
Ein Freund hat dir diesen Flyer gegeben. Du zeigst ihn deinen Eltern. Beantworte ihre Fragen.

1. Wo ist die Surfschule? ______
2. Wann findet der Unterricht statt? ______
3. Was muss man können, um teilzunehmen? ______
4. Ab welchem Alter kann man teilnehmen? ______
5. Wieviel kostet das? ______

______

2 (MEDIATION) At the surf school

44/1

Du hast deine Eltern überzeugt und darfst surfen lernen. Deine Eltern begleiten dich zur ersten Stunde. Vermittle zwischen ihnen und dem Surflehrer.

Instructor: Welcome! I hope you enjoy your first lesson!
You: Thank you! This is my mum and dad. They have got some questions.
Instructor: Hi! How can I help you?
Your dad: Heute sind die Wellen sehr groß. Frag ihn, ob das gefährlich ist.

You: ______

Instructor: No, the first lesson is on the beach. And we will be careful when we go into the water.

You: ______

______

Your mum: Was passiert, wenn es einen Unfall gibt?

You: ______

Instructor: There is a doctor in the village. But don't worry, everything will be fine!

You: ______

Ziel 1: I can understand information about free-time activities in Wales.

→ ⦾ h6t697

The Brecon Beacons

If you like hiking, you should visit the Brecon Beacons. It is a huge park in the middle of Wales with mountains, caves, museums and an adventure farm. The park is great if you like hiking. All you need are some strong shoes and a map (and maybe a coat). You can take a picnic and enjoy walking through the woods, up mountains and along rivers. It is a great place for all ages.

Answer the questions.

1. What is the Brecon Beacons?

____

2. What can you find in the park?

____

3. What equipment do you need if you want to go hiking?

____

4. What else can you do?

____

____

5. What age should you be?

____

5P

→p. 38/1

Ziel 2: I can present information about a sport.

→ ⦾ bk85ct → ⦾ mg6ex4

Write about a sport you want to try. Think about the following things:

What's the sport like? What do you do?
What equipment do you need? Why do you want to try it?

____

____

____

____

____

____

____

7P

→p. 38/2

Ziel 3: I can make an emergency call.

→ ⦾ hh8aw7 → ⦾ p2kq6y

Read the information below and write a dialogue for an emergency call.

Service?	**How?**
ambulance	hot water
Who?	**Where?**
your brother Jayden	at home
What's the problem?	15 Penylan Road, Cardiff
burnt hand	

Man: Hello, which service please?

You: I need ______________________________

Man: Hello, this is the ambulance service. What's the problem?

You: Hello. It's ______________________________

____

Man: Ok, how did that happen?

You: ______________________________

Man: Where are are you?

You: ______________________________

Man: The ambulance ______________________________

5P

→ p. 39/3

Ziel 4: I can understand a report from a school website.

→ ⦾ rs94db

Read the text on pages 42–43 in your book again and answer the questions.

1. What did the class visit?

____

2. What is Caldicot Castle?

____

____

3. Who is Lancelot?

____

4. What did the students learn?

____

5. When did the knight have to go to the stocks?

____

6. What did the students think about the trip?

____

6P

→ p. 39/4

Ziel 5: I can pass on information about a free-time activity.

a) Lies dir den Flyer durch und beantworte die Fragen auf Deutsch.

Learn to ski in Cardiff!

Skiing in the centre of the city? Of course!
Ice Arena Wales has an indoor ski centre with real snow.
You don't need to worry about the weather or if there will be enough snow here! You can ski seven days a week all year round.
There are lessons for all ages, or you can just come and practise by yourself.
You can buy or rent equipment in our shop, but please wear warm clothes.
After skiing you can relax in our café or restaurant.

Skiing is great exercise and a fun activity. Try it today!

1. Wo befindet sich die Ice Arena? ______
2. Was gibt es dort? ______
3. Wie kann man dort Skifahren lernen? ______
4. Muss man die Ausrüstung mitbringen? ______
5. Gibt es auch etwas zu essen dort? ______

b) Du bist mit einer Freundin, die nicht gut Englisch kann, am Eingang der Ice Arena. Sie hat ein paar Fragen. Vermittle zwischen ihr und einer Mitarbeiterin der Ice Arena.

Your friend: Kannst du sie fragen, ob es da drin sehr kalt ist?

You: ______

Woman: Yes, it is. You need warm clothes.

You: ______

Your friend: Frag sie, ob ich eine Jacke ausleihen kann.

You: ______

Woman: ______

______

You: Nein, man kann nur die Ausrüstung zum Skifahren ausleihen. Aber es gibt in der Nähe ein Sportgeschäft.

9P

→ p. 39/5

Lösungen online
69n2if

○ **Ziel 1: I can understand information about free-time activities in Wales.**

Read the texts and complete the sentences.

Wales is a great place to go horse riding. Welsh horses are very friendly. You can borrow horses and equipment at the horse riding schools.

You can try many different water sports in Wales. Canoeing, surfing and rafting are very popular activities.

Lifeboats are very important in Wales. They help people at sea. People on lifeboats are usually volunteers.

A lot of people in Wales speak Welsh. You can also find Welsh on menus and road signs.

1. You can borrow horses and equipment ______________________________ .
2. You can try ______________________________ in Wales.
3. Popular activities are ______________________________ .
4. Lifeboats are important because ______________________________ .
5. People on lifeboats ______________________________ .
6. You can find Welsh ______________________________ .

○ **Ziel 2: I can present information about a sport.**

Write a text about a sport you like.

I like ____________________ .

It is ______________________________ .

It is ____________________ to learn.

You must be ______________________________ .

You need ______________________________ .

football | tennis | netball | ...
exciting | fast | cool | ...
dangerous | easy | difficult | ...
strong | fast | careful | clever | ...
sports clothes | ball | helmet | ...

○ **Ziel 3: I can make an emergency call.**

Put the dialogue in the correct order.

☐ In 15 Wood Street, Cardiff.
☐ Hello, this is the ambulance service. What's the problem?
☐ It's Ryan Wall. My number is 07852 1767349.
☐ Ambulance, please.
☐ OK, an ambulance is coming. Can you tell me your name and phone number?
☐ There has been a car accident. A man has hurt his head. He is bleeding.
☐ Hello, which service do you need?
☐ Thank you. Please stay there until the ambulance arrives.
☐ Can you tell me where you are, please?

○ **Ziel 4: I can understand a report from a school website.**

Read the text on pages 42–43 in your book again and put a circle around the right words.

1. Caldicot Castle in Wales is over 1,100 • 900 • 500 years old.
2. The guide was a teacher • a student • a knight.
3. The castle had dark corridors and tall towers • a huge kitchen • a playground.
4. The class learnt how to joust • cook • dance.
5. When they were naughty, knights had to go to the tower • stocks • castle wall.
6. The class learned lots about the castle • Mr Yeates • their guide.

○ **Ziel 5: I can pass on information about a free-time activity.**

Lies dir den Flyer durch und beantworte die Fragen auf Deutsch.

1. Wann finden der Tennisunterricht statt?

____

2. Wie alt muss man sein?

____

3. Wo findet der Kurs statt?

____

4. Wie kann man sich anmelden?

____

Tennis Lessons!

Every Saturday morning 9–11 a.m.
Ages from 5–16
In Manor House Park
Friendly instructors
Have fun and make new friends!

Call Jane on 02035 778589

51/3

1 Collect information for a film review.

a) Choose a film you like and answer the questions.

1. What's the title of the film?

____

2. What is the story about?

____

____

3. Where is the location of the film?

____

4. Who are the actors in the film?

____

____

5. What is the ending of the film?

____

____

b) Make a mind map for your review.

→ Collect ideas and words before you start to write.

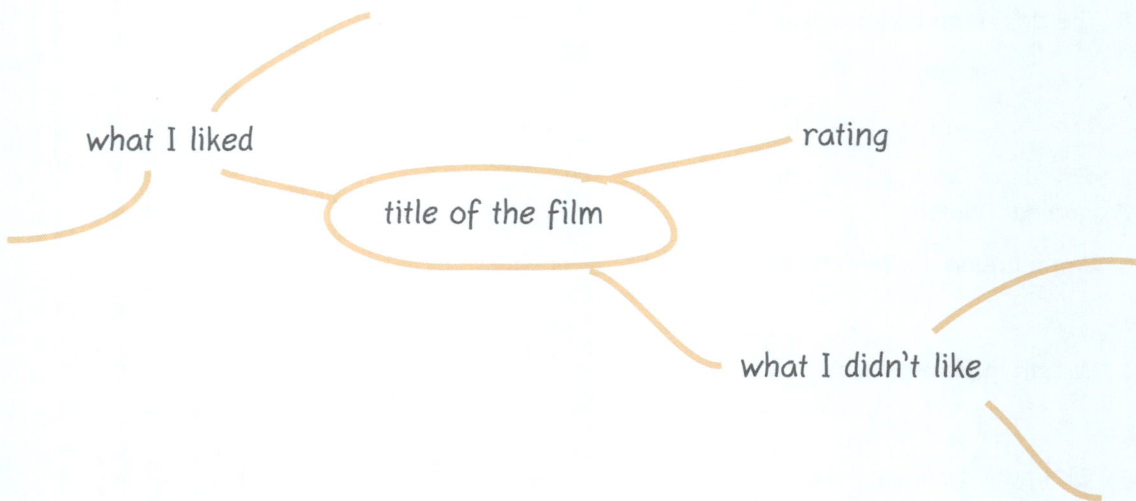

51/3

2 Use the information from exercise 1 and write a review of the film.

51/3

3 Read your review to the class and ask for feedback.

a) Did you understand what the film is about?

b) How many people would like to watch the film?

c) Why / why not?

To find out the writer's opinion look at the rating and the words (adjectives ...).

A

Do you love animals?
Be a volunteer!

Swansea animal rescue shelter needs more volunteers to help them look after the animals at their shelter. You can do as many hours as you like and they need people seven days a week. You can choose to walk dogs, play with cats, clean cages or work in the office. If you think you can help, visit their website.

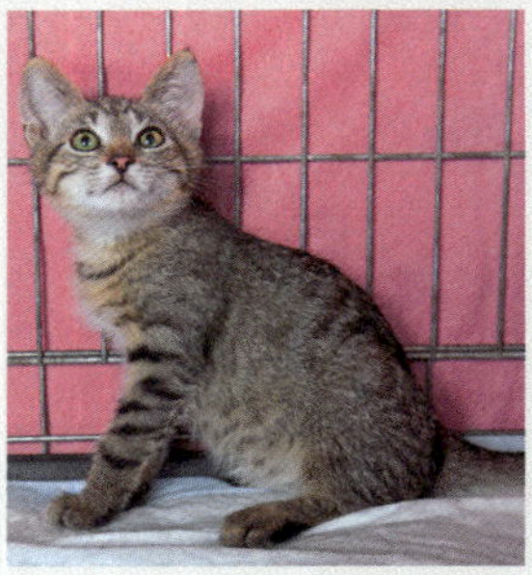

B

New film club for teenagers

From next Thursday a new film club for teenagers will meet every week in Abergavenny town hall. We are going to watch films from Wales. The first film will be 'Submarine'. After the club has watched the film, there will be time to talk about it and enjoy some snacks. Michael Gould, who has started the group said, "Everyone is welcome. We hope teenagers will like to watch some of the great films from Wales, learn more about their country and make new friends". The club meets at 7 p.m.

C

Abergavenny's under 15 basketball team wins again!

Dai Morgan, the boss of Abergavenny's basketball team, was very happy after his under 15 team won 55–47 against Cardiff. Star player Gareth Morris made 22 points in a fast and exciting match. After the match Dai Morgan said, "It was a great game and the boys played well. I'm proud of them." Their next match will be on Saturday. Everyone is welcome to come and watch.

D

Lake canoeing trip

Why not go on a North Wales canoeing trip next month? We will visit the beautiful Gweryd Lakes for a day trip for people who have gone canoeing before and who are new to canoeing.
The trip is £40 for the bus and an instructor. You can borrow equipment if you need to. Bring a picnic and enjoy the beautiful lakes. Call 07715 2391122

READING

1 Read the four texts. Which activity can you choose if you ...

1. love animals? ☐
2. like watching sport? ☐
3. like being in the countryside? ☐
4. like films? ☐

2 Find words or phrases from the text for the pictures.

1. ______________________

2. ______________________

3. ______________________

4. ______________________

5. ______________________

6. ______________________

3 Underline the right ending to finish the sentence.

1. The animal rescue shelter needs more… a) dogs. b) volunteers. c) cages.
2. The film club is going to watch films from … a) Wales. b) Germany. c) France.
3. The next basketball match will be … a) next week. b) next month. c) on Saturday.
4. The lake canoeing trip will take … a) a day. b) two days. c) a week.

4 Read the text again and answer the questions.

1. How many hours can the volunteers work at the animal shelter?

____

2. What can the volunteers do at the animal shelter?

____

3. When does the film club for teenagers meet?

____

4. What did the boss of Abergavenny's basketball team say after the match?

____

5. How much is the canoeing trip?

____

6. Do you have to bring your own equipment for the canoeing trip?

____

Unit 3

Made in Scotland

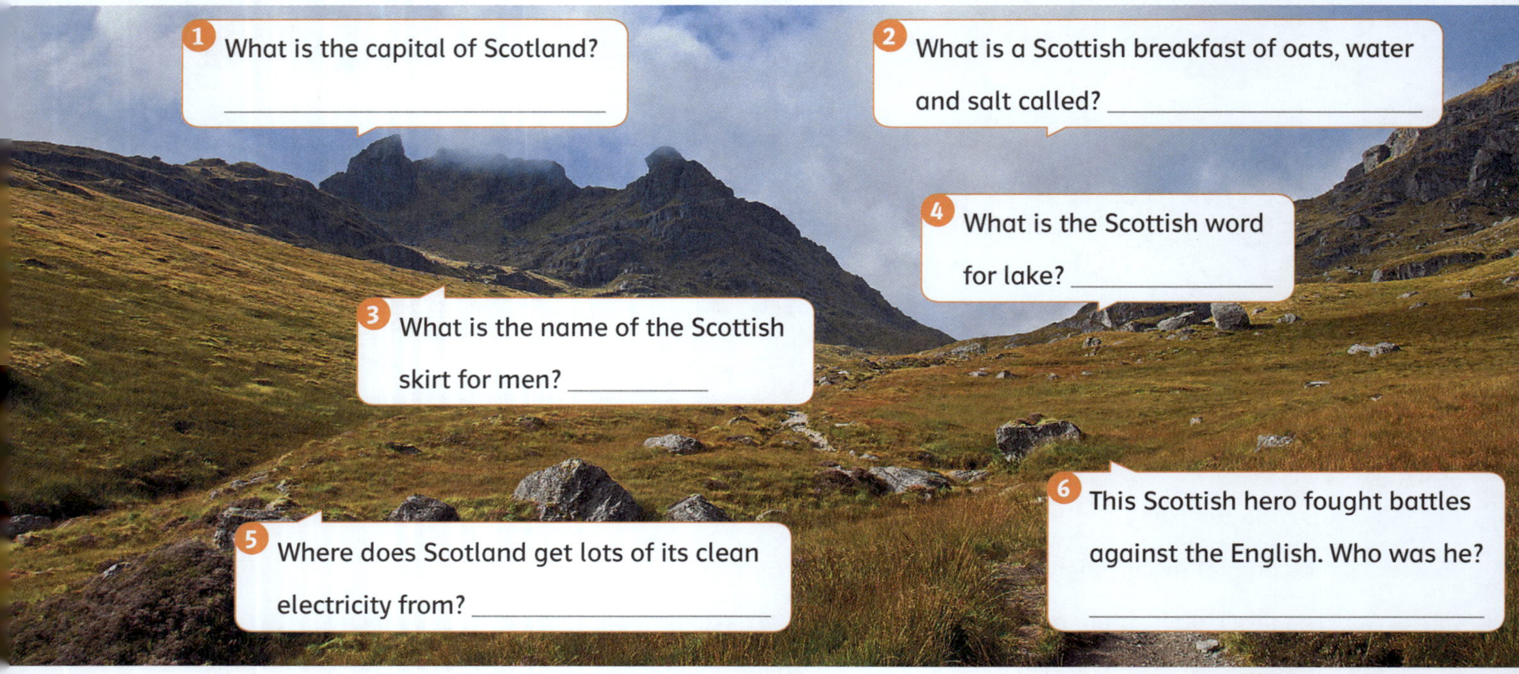

52/2

1 Information about Scotland

a) Write the answers to the questions.

b) Look at the pictures on page 52–53 in your book. Would you like to visit Scotland? Why / why not? Write five sentences or more in your exercise book.

6 53/3

2 (LISTENING) Listen to Katie and her friend Ben. Tick the right box.

1. Katie is going on holiday to …
   a) Scotland. ☐ b) England. ☐ c) Wales. ☐
2. Ben went to Scotland …
   a) last year. ☐ b) two years ago. ☐ c) last week. ☐
3. Ben stayed …
   a) in a hotel. ☐ b) in a cottage. ☐ c) in a tent. ☐
4. Ben visited …
   a) Edinburgh and a museum. ☐ b) Edinburgh and the countryside. ☐ c) a museum and a loch. ☐
5. Ben saw a man …
   a) in a restaurant. ☐ b) with bagpipes. ☐ c) with a Scottish flag. ☐

1 Find the words.

54/1

1. Both Bell's mother and his **e f i w** couldn't hear well. ______________
2. The inventor moved to Boston and opened a school for **a d e f** people. ______________
3. His **a b i i m n o t** was to make a machine which changed sounds to electricity. ______________
4. Alexander Graham Bell invented the **e e e h l n o p t** in 1876. ______________
5. Bell's invention was a big **e c c s s s u** and he became rich. ______________

2 Materials

/5a)

a) Write the names of the materials under the pictures.

b) Find examples of things which are made of these materials.

1. leather: shoes
2. ______________
3. ______________
4. ______________

5. ______________
6. ______________
7. ______________
8. ______________

3 What are these things often made of? Complete the sentences.

/5b)

1. Scarves are often made of ______________ .
2. Dresses are often made of ______________ .
3. Bridges are often made of ______________ .
4. Buildings are often made of ______________ .
5. Planes are often made of ______________ .
6. Boxes are often made of ______________ .
7. Cups and plates are often made of ______________ .

4 Who or which? Underline the right word.

56/8

1. Scots are people which • who come from Scotland.
2. Porridge is something for breakfast which • who is made with oats.
3. Edinburgh is a city which • who is famous for its inventors.
4. Alexander Graham Bell was an inventor which • who was born in Edinburgh.
5. Loch Ness is a lake which • who is famous for its monster.
6. Nessie is a monster which • who lives in Loch Ness.
7. Robert the Bruce is a Scottish hero which • who was born in 1274.
8. The kilt is a kind of skirt which • who men wear in Scotland.

5 Use who or which to make one sentence out of two.

56/9a)

1. Scotland is a part of the United Kingdom. It had its own king or queen in the past.
   Scotland is a part of the United Kingdom which had its own king or queen in the past.
   ____
2. Edinburgh is a Scottish city. It's famous for its inventors.
   ____
   ____
3. Alexander Graham Bell was an inventor. He invented the telephone.
   ____
   ____
4. Edinburgh is a very old city. It has always produced new ideas.
   ____
   ____
5. Scotland is a very windy place. It isn't very sunny.
   ____
6. 'Loch' is a Scottish word. It means lake.
   ____
7. Porridge is a Scottish dish. It is made with oats, water and salt.
   ____
   ____
8. Robert the Bruce is a Scottish hero. He fought against the English.
   ____
   ____

6 Write sentences with who or which.

/9a)

a) Complete the sentences.

1. Edinburgh is famous for its inventors.
   Edinburgh is a city which is famous for its inventors.
2. John Dunlop invented a better tyre.
   John Dunlop is the man ______
3. A coat keeps you warm in winter.
   A coat is a thing ______
4. A doctor helps sick people.
   A doctor is a person ______
5. Sharks live in the sea.
   Sharks are animals ______
6. A nurse works in a hospital.
   A nurse is a person ______

/9b)

b) Use the words and write three more sentences in your exercise book.

a knight | a bird | a wind farm

10a)

7 Write sentences with whose.

a) Write sentences about Tina's friends.

1. Luna's mother is a hairdresser.
   I have a friend whose mother is a hairdresser.
2. Ella's mother is a doctor.
   I have a friend ______
3. Sarah's father is an actor.
   I have a friend ______
4. Pia's brother is a baker.
   I have a friend ______
5. Jacob's father is a builder.
   I have a friend ______
6. Finn's sister is an engineer.
   I have a friend ______

b) Write three more sentences about your friends in your exercise book.

8 Write sentences with whose.

57/10a)

1. Percy Spencer
2. Alexander Graham Bell
3. John A. Miller
4. John Logie Baird
5. Charles Seeberger

1. Percy Spencer is the man whose invention was the microwave.
2. Alexander Graham Bell ______
3. ______
4. ______
5. ______

9 Match the sentence parts and put in who or whose.

57/10b)

1. An inventor is someone who ______
2. A teacher is someone ______
3. A chef is someone ______
4. A vet is someone ______
5. A baker is someone ______
6. A doctor is someone ______
7. A zookeeper is someone ______
8. A director is someone ______

- job it is to look after animals.
- job it is to make bread and cakes.
- tells the actors how to act in a film.
- works in a school.
- job it is to cook food for people.
- helps when your pet is ill.
- job it is to look after people who are ill or hurt.
- has ideas and makes new things.

10 (WRITING) Write a biography about yourself.

57/11

was born | grew up | started school | spent holiday | started sport | father / mother works as a … | brother / sister was born in … | …

______
______
______
______
______
______
______
______

58/2

1 Use the verbs to make the gerund.

1. Mum loves ________________ (cook).
2. ________________ (shop) for clothes is my favourite activity.
3. I think ________________ (hike) is boring.
4. Jake hates ________________ (tidy) up after breakfast.

5. ________________ (spend) a few days in Edinburgh is a good idea.
6. Katie doesn't like ________________ (camp).
7. I like ________________ my bike at weekends.

9/3a)

2 What are the words?

1. A cheap place where young people stay: ________________
2. A small holiday house which you can rent: ________________
3. It has a lot of rooms and large buffets: ________________
4. A place where you go camping: ________________
5. A place that is almost like home: ________________
6. A small home which a car can pull: ________________

9/3a)

3 Find the words.

a) Find the words in the word search and complete the sentences.

1. Dad says camping is ________________ and cheap.
2. Mum would like to stay in a ________________ B&B.
3. Jake hates ________________ .
4. Mum wants to get tips about ________________ food.
5. Katie thinks hotels are very ________________ and that the food is ________________ .
6. Dad wants to go ________________ .

X	U	P	T	B	Z	A	J	O	R	U
N	C	B	S	I	M	P	L	E	B	S
N	B	I	R	B	B	B	O	B	O	M
I	U	O	B	C	Y	B	C	I	L	E
C	O	M	F	O	R	T	A	B	L	E
E	B	F	M	S	B	B	L	B	Y	C
B	I	O	B	Y	U	B	G	K	S	O
I	N	S	E	C	T	S	W	F	T	T
T	U	J	H	I	K	I	N	G	D	J

9/3b)

b) Put in the missing words.

1. We'll have to m________________ for our hotel soon. Let's have a look online.
2. This one looks nice. We can't c________________ before two in the afternoon.
3. We have to c________________ by 10 a.m. It says that we can only p________________ with cash.

4 (LISTENING) Listen to Jake and Katie and tick the right box.

7 59/4

	right	wrong	not in the text
1. Katie wants to stay in a hotel or a castle.	☐	☐	☐
2. Katie has bought new boots for her holiday.	☐	☐	☐
3. Katie wants to stay with another family.	☐	☐	☐
4. Jake likes porridge.	☐	☐	☐
5. Katie wants to stay near Loch Ness.	☐	☐	☐
6. There is a great hotel near Loch Ness.	☐	☐	☐
7. They would like to sell a picture of Nessie.	☐	☐	☐

5 Complete the sentences.

60/5

1. If Dad wants (want) to go camping, we'll stay at a campsite.
2. If I _______ (go) camping, I'll freeze.
3. If we ___________ (stay) at a campsite, we'll be outside all day.
4. If Jake ____________ (wear) a kilt, we'll all laugh.
5. If it ___________ (rain), we'll visit a museum.
6. If it ______ (be) sunny, we won't visit a museum.
7. If you ___________ (have) time, you'll go to Loch Ness.
8. If they __________ (see) the Loch Ness monster, they will take lots of pictures.

6 Complete the sentences.

60/5

1. If we stay at a campsite, we 'll meet (meet) lots of young people.
2. If we go camping, we _________________ (need) nice weather.
3. If we stay at a B & B, we ________________ (get) a good breakfast.
4. If we stay at a B & B, the people __________________ (give) us some tips about things to do.
5. If we go to a hotel, there ___________________ (not be) any insects.
6. If we don't stay at a hotel, we ____________________ (not get) nice food.
7. We _________________ (have) our own bathroom if we stay at a hotel.
8. Maybe we ________________ (see) the Loch Ness monster if we go to Loch Ness.

7 Put in the right form of the verb.

0/6a)

1. We *won't have* (not have) a problem with insects if we ________ (stay) in a hotel.
2. If Mum ________ (not want) to go camping, we ________ (not stay) at a campsite.
3. If we ________ (go) to Edinburgh, we ________ (visit) a museum.
4. Katie ________ (take) a picture if she ________ (see) a man in a kilt.
5. If we ________ (have) internet, we ________ (look) for some tips about things to do.
6. Katie ________ (try) porridge if we ________ (stay) at a hotel.
7. If there ________ (be) a breakfast buffet, Jake ________ (eat) too much.
8. Dad ________ (be) very happy if we ________ (go) hiking with him.

8 Write your own sentences.

0/6b)

1. If I go to Scotland, ________
2. If I don't stay at a hotel, ________
3. If the weather is good, ________
4. If I go hiking, ________
5. If it rains, ________
6. If the food isn't good, ________

9 Look at the pictures and complete the sentences.

61/7

1 If we go on holiday this year, …

2 If we want to see a nice city, …

3 We'll have a good breakfast if …

4 If we go shopping, …

5 We won't go to Loch Ness if …

6 If we go to Loch Ness, …

1. ________
2. ________
3. ________
4. ________
5. ________
6. ________

❀ 10 (WRITING) A trip to Scotland

61/9

a) You are planning a trip to Scotland with your aunt. You have found a hostel where you would like to stay. Read the information on the website.

INTERNET

THE HOSTEL | BOOKING | FAQS | BLOG | CONTACT

HAGGIS HOSTEL

PLACE: Bread Street, Edinburgh, 5 minutes to city centre

ACTIVITIES: museums, restaurants, theatre, shopping

PRICE: £112 for 2 people for 2 nights, breakfast included

b) Your aunt has sent you this e-mail. Read her e-mail.

E-MAIL

Re: Our trip

Hi!

I think I've found the best hotel! It's in the centre of Edinburgh and looks very cosy. It has a fantastic breakfast buffet! It's a bit expensive – it costs £350 for a double room for 2 nights. Is that OK with you? When we are in Edinburgh, we can go shopping and go to museums. I love shopping! Where should we go after Edinburgh? Inverness? If you like, we'll go on a boat trip on Loch Ness. Let me know what you think about the hotel.

See you soon! Alice

c) Write an answer to her e-mail. You can use the following phrases.

- Let's go to ...
- ... is cheaper / more expensive.
- I would like to ...
- If you like ..., you will / won't like ...
- That's (not) a good / bad idea.
- I prefer ...
- I think so too. / I agree / disagree.
- I like / don't like ..., so ... is better for me.

1 (LISTENING) Spell the words.

8 · 61/9

a) Listen to the words and write them.

1. ______ 5. ______
2. ______ 6. ______
3. ______ 7. ______
4. ______ 8. ______

b) Write down three words and a telephone number. Spell the words and say the number to your partner. Write down the words and number they tell you in your exercise book.

1. ______ 3. ______
2. ______ 4. ______

2 (SPEAKING) Talk about inventions.

61/9

a) Think of an invention. Don't tell your partner what it is. Your partner tries to find out what the invention is. Use the phrases below.

Is it made of metal / plastic / wood / … ? | Yes, it is. / No, it isn't. | Is it black / white / brown / … ? | Do people use it to talk / … ? | Yes, they do. / No, they don't. | …

b) Think of other inventions and act more dialogues with your partner.

3 (SPEAKING) Edinburgh or Loch Ness?

61/9

a) Where would you like to visit? Look at the pictures and the information below about the two places. Then talk to your partner and decide together which place you would like to visit.

Edinburgh

Loch Ness

Edinburgh: hotel / B & B | city | shops | castle | museum | weather | photos | sights | public transport

Loch Ness: campsite | insects | the Highlands | castle | mountains | weather | photos | countryside | hiking

b) Think of two other places (they can be in Germany). Collect information and show it to your partner. Decide together which place you would like to visit.

65/6

1 (READING) Read the comic strip.

The Battle of Bannockburn

2 Answer the questions.

65/6

1. Where are the soldiers?

____

2. Why aren't the soldiers happy?

____

3. What happens during the battle?

____

4. What happens to the soldier with the injury?

____

5. Why are all the Scottish soldiers happy after the battle?

____

3 (WRITING) Write a story about the Battle of Bannockburn.

65/6

a) Use the comic strip above and the comic strip in your book on pages 62–65 for help. Write notes.

When?	Who?	What?	Why?

b) Write the story in your exercise book.

The Battle of Bannockburn was in 1314.

Scones

225 g flour
1 tablespoon of baking powder
1 pinch of salt
55 g butter
25 g sugar
150 ml milk
1 egg, beaten

Heat the oven to 220°C.
Mix together the flour, baking powder, salt and rub in the butter with your fingers. Stir in the sugar and then the milk to make a soft dough.
Put the dough on a floured work surface and knead very lightly. Pat out until it is 2 cm thick. Use a round cutter to cut out the scones and place on a baking sheet. Brush the tops of the scones with the beaten egg. Bake for 12–15 minutes until golden.

Serve with butter and jam.

Kalter Hund

250 g Kokosfett
7 EL Puderzucker
4 EL Kakaopulver
2 Päckchen Vanillezucker
2 Eier
2 Packungen Butterkekse

Die Eier mit dem Puderzucker und dem Vanillezucker schaumig rühren. Den Kakao zugeben und alles verrühren.
Das Kokosfett in einem Topf so lange erhitzen, bis es flüssig ist. Einige Zeit auskühlen lassen.
Das Kokosfett unter die Kakao-Mischung geben und gut verrühren.
Eine Kastenform mit Frischhaltefolie auslegen und den Boden dünn mit der Creme bestreichen. Abwechselnd die Butterkekse mit der Creme einschichten.
Den Kalten Hund für ein paar Stunden in den Kühlschrank stellen.

66/1

1 (MEDIATION) Beantworte die Fragen.

Ein Deutscher und eine Schottin haben diese Rezepte gesehen, aber sie verstehen sie nicht ganz. Beantworte ihre Fragen in der jeweiligen Sprache.

1. Welche Zutaten braucht man für Scones?
____
2. Wie lange und bei wieviel Grad muss man die Scones backen?
____
3. Womit isst man die Scones?
____
4. 'Kalter Hund' means cold dog! What's in it? Dog meat?
____
5. I'm a vegetarian and I don't eat eggs. Can I eat 'Kalter Hund'?
____
6. I can see the word 'Kühlschrank'. Don't you have to put the cake in the oven?
____

Ziel 1: I can understand information about Scotland. → ⦾ 3vu9jw

A Scottish band

Marie Stuart has lived in the Scottish countryside near Aberdeen all her life. She plays the bagpipes. Forty years ago Marie's father started a band and today there are about thirty people in it. The band plays Scottish music. Marie and the other people in the band all wear kilts and jackets and play together every week. Their music is very loud so it's a good thing the neighbours live a few miles away. The band plays at concerts, weddings and parties. They have won many prizes and they have even met the Queen!

Answer the questions.

1. Where does Marie live? ______
2. What does she play? ______
3. Who started the band? ______
4. What do the people in the band wear? ______
5. What kind of music does the band play? ______
6. How often does the band meet? ______
7. Where does the band play? ______
8. Which famous person has the band met? ______

8P
→ p. 60/1

Ziel 2: I can present information about an inventor. → ⦾ 73qw9c → ⦾ 4qb3fw

Write a short text about the inventor John Logie Baird. Use the information in the box.

______
______
______
______
______
______
______
______

John Logie Baird

14th August 1888–14th June 1946
engineer near Glasgow
moved to the south of England in 1922
started work on a TV
world's first TV in 1926

5P
→ p. 60/2

Ziel 3: I can talk about different kinds of holidays.

→ ⦾ 9u4p9d → ⦾ s5ip98

You are going to go on holiday to Scotland with your friend. You want to go to Edinburgh, but your friend wants to go camping at Loch Ness. Use the words below and complete the dialogue.

Loch Ness | be in the countryside | go shopping | cheaper | really interesting | youth hostel near Loch Ness | at a nice hotel | sounds great | hate insects

Your friend: I'd really like to go to ____________________ !

You: But Edinburgh is ____________________ .

Your friend: Loch Ness is interesting too!

You: I'd like to ____________________ ! And I want to stay ____________________ .

Your friend: But camping is ____________________ ! And it's nice to ____________________ .

You: Yes, but I ____________________ !

Your friend: OK, let's go to Edinburgh first and then find a ____________________ .

You: OK, that ____________________ !

9P

→ p. 60/3

Ziel 4: I can understand a comic strip about a battle.

→ ⦾ q8e3fp

Read the story about Robert the Bruce on pages 62–65 in your book again. Answer the questions.

1. When Robert the Bruce became king in 1306, what did he want to do?

   ____

2. How many battles did he lose?

   ____

3. Where did Robert the Bruce hide?

   ____

4. What did he see in the cave?

   ____

5. What did Robert learn from the spider?

   ____

6. Why did the Scots win the battle?

   ____

7. Why did the Scots love King Robert the Bruce?

   ____

7P

→ p. 61/4

Ziel 5: I can pass on information about food.

Fish and chips

Fish and chips is a very popular takeaway dish in Scotland. The fish is covered in batter, deep fried in hot oil and served with chips. If you don't like the batter, you don't have to eat it. The person who serves you will ask if you want salt and vinegar over everything. Say, "No, thanks." if you don't want it! You can also have ketchup. You will find chip shops or 'chippies' in almost every town in the United Kingdom – and you can find the best chip shops near harbours. The fish is very fresh there – it's juicy and delicious and tastes best when you eat it out of the paper while it's still hot. But you don't have to order fish in a chip shop – you can also order deep fried sausage, deep fried pizza or even deep fried chocolate!

a) Lies den Text und beantworte die Fragen auf Deutsch.

1. Wie wird Fish und Chips zubereitet?

____

2. Kann man Fish and Chips nur mit Salz und Essig essen?

____

3. Wo findet man die besten Fish and Chips-Läden?

____

4. Gibt es dort nur Fish and Chips?

____

____

b) Du bist mit deiner Familie in einem Fish and Chips-Laden. Vermittle zwischen deiner Mutter und dem Verkäufer.

Your mum: Kannst du bitte fragen wie frisch der Fisch ist?

You: ______________________________

Man: It's very fresh. I caught it this morning.

You: ______________________________

Your mum: Und kann ich Ketchup zu den Pommes haben?

You: ______________________________

Man: Yes, of course.

You: ______________________________

8P

→ p. 61/5

Lösungen online
7k2eh9

○ Ziel 1: I can understand information about people and places in Scotland.

A Scottish Band

Marie Stuart has lived in the Scottish countryside near Aberdeen all her life. She plays the bagpipes. Forty years ago Marie's father started a band which plays Scottish music on the bagpipes. Today there are about thirty people in the band. They play every week. The music is very loud! It's good that the neighbours live a few miles away. All the players wear kilts, jackets and hats. They play at concerts, weddings and other events. They win many prizes and they have even met the Queen!

Tick the right box.

	right	wrong
1. Marie has lived in the Scottish countryside all her life.	☐	☐
2. Marie plays the bagpipes.	☐	☐
3. Marie started a band forty years ago.	☐	☐
4. There are about forty people in the band.	☐	☐
5. They play every week.	☐	☐
6. All the players wear kilts.	☐	☐

○ Ziel 2: I can present information about an inventor.

Complete the biography of John Dunlop.

John Dunlop was born ______________________________

______________ . He worked as ______________________ .

In 1867 he ______________________ . He presented his

______________________ . In 1889 he ____________

______________________ . John Dunlop died ____________

______________ .

John Dunlop

in Scotland on 5th February 1840
a vet in Edinburgh
to Ireland in 1867
his tyre with air in 1888
his own company in 1889
on 23rd October 1921

○ Ziel 3: I can talk about different kinds of holidays.

Put the dialogue in the right order.

☐ Yes, but Loch Ness is interesting too. You will like it there.

☐ OK. That sounds great.

☐ Edinburgh is a really interesting city. I would like to stay there.

☐ Yes, that's a good idea. Is it expensive to stay in Edinburgh?

☐ Yes, it is. But we can stay at a youth hostel. It's cheaper than a hotel.

☐ Let's go to Edinburgh first and then go camping at Loch Ness.

○ **Ziel 4: I can understand a comic strip about a battle.**

Read the text on pages 62–65 in your book again. Tick the right box.

	right	wrong
1. The English wanted to have Scotland.	☐	☐
2. Robert the Bruce was the King of England.	☐	☐
3. Robert the Bruce wanted to keep the English out.	☐	☐
4. In 1316 Edward I was the King of England.	☐	☐
5. Robert the Bruce won six battles.	☐	☐
6. King Edward died at the Battle of Bannockburn in 1314.	☐	☐
7. The English had more soldiers than the Scots.	☐	☐
8. The Scots won because they knew the land.	☐	☐

○ **Ziel 5: I can pass on information about food.**

Porridge

Porridge is a warm dish with oats, water and salt. It is one of the most popular breakfasts in Scotland, especially during the cold winters. There are many different recipes for porridge. Many people think that you can only cook real porridge with water and a pinch of salt. Others prefer to cook the oats in a mixture of water and milk.

Lies den Text und beantworte die Fragen auf Deutsch.

1. Wo isst man gerne Porridge zum Frühstück?

____

2. Wann wird gerne Porridge gegessen?

____

3. Gibt es ein bestimmtes Rezept für Porridge?

____

4. Kochen alle Leute Porridge mit Milch?

____

Greyfriar's Bobby

In the old town of Edinburgh there is a statue of a skye terrier. The little dog is called Greyfriar's Bobby. Bobby is Scotland's most famous dog.

John Gray was a police officer and Bobby was his dog. Together they walked around the streets of Edinburgh because they wanted to keep people safe. One day John became very ill and in 1858 he died. They buried him in the churchyard at Greyfriars Church. The little dog came to the churchyard and sat next to his master's grave every day, even in rain or snow. The caretaker of the church tried to keep Bobby away, but Bobby came back every day.

His story touched the people of Edinburgh and they built a shelter for him next to John's grave. The people who knew Bobby looked after him well. He sat at his master's grave for fourteen years until he died in 1872 at the age of 16. The people buried him close to John Gray.

The statue of Bobby is very popular. Visitors from all over the world come there to hear Bobby's story and take pictures of his statue. Everyone loves the amazing story of the most faithful dog in Scotland.

73/2

1 Look at the dictionary entry.

a) Read the dictionary entry for 'touch'.

touch [tʌtʃ] **I.** *n* <*pl* -es> ① Berührung *f*; **at the ~ of a button** auf Knopfdruck ② *no pl (ability to feel)* Tasten *nt;* **the sense of ~** der Tastsinn ③ *no pl (communication)* Kontakt *m;* **to be in ~ with sb/sth** mit jdm/etw in Kontakt sein **II.** *vt* ① berühren, anfassen ② *(move emotionally)* bewegen ▶ **to ~ a** [**raw**] **nerve** einen wunden Punkt berühren **III.** *vi* berühren
◆ **touch down** *vi* AVIAT landen
◆ **touch off** *vt* auslösen
◆ **touch on**, **touch upon** *vi* ansprechen
◆ **touch up** *vt* ① *(improve)* auffrischen; *photograph* retuschieren ② BRIT *(fam: assault sexually)* **to ~ sb up** jdn begrapschen *pej*

The words in a dictionary are in groups or 'entries'. Each entry has a root word. Look for the root word first.

This part tells you how to say the word.

Here you can see if the word is a verb, noun, an adjective, …

In the entry you can find useful phrases.

Many words have more than one meaning. There is a number for each meaning.

These words help you find the right meaning.

b) Use the entry for 'touch' to find the right German word(s) in these sentences:

1. The story of Greyfriars Bobby touches everyone who hears it. ______________
2. We'll be in touch. ______________
3. You can open the box at the touch of a button. ______________
4. The little dog touched the girl with his nose. ______________

73/2

2 Put the underlined words from the text in alphabetical order.

1. ______________ 4. ______________
2. ______________ 5. ______________
3. ______________ 6. ______________

73/2

3 Work with a dictionary.

Find the right German word or words. Use an English-German dictionary.

1. In the old town of Edinburgh there is a <u>statue</u> of a little dog. ______________
2. They <u>buried</u> him. ______________
3. They buried him in the <u>churchyard</u>. ______________
4. They built a <u>shelter</u> for him next to John's grave. ______________
5. Everyone loves the amazing story of the most <u>faithful</u> dog in Scotland. ______________

73/2

4 More words from the text

Which other words in the text don't you understand? Write them down and find their meanings in your dictionary.

English word	German word

Du kannst auch online Wörterbücher benutzen. Pass aber auf. Nimm nicht gleich die erstbeste Bedeutung. Lies erst den gesamten Eintrag. Du kannst auch die Bedeutung in deinem Deutsch-Englisch Wörterbuch gegenprüfen.

Last year I went on holiday with my family to Scotland. First we stayed in Edinburgh for a few days, and then we drove north and stayed at a nice cottage at Loch Ness. The cottage was so close to the lake that I could see it from my bedroom window. There were lots of books about Nessie, the Loch Ness monster, and we read all about it. And, of course, we all wanted to see it too. Everyone except my mum who said it was "a joke"!

Every day after breakfast we went for a long walk along the loch. I carried my phone in my hand so that I could take a photo or make a video when I saw Nessie. Once, my dad thought he could see it. There was something in the lake, but it was quite far away. I could see it too. The thing swam closer and then we saw that it was only a big black dog. Mum laughed.

The holiday was over too quickly and we had to go home. We packed everything in the car. I felt sad – I really believed there was a monster in the loch. I went for one last walk. And that's when I saw it! Suddenly something moved in the water. It was black and huge! I made a video on my phone.

Then I ran back to the cottage and shouted: "I saw it! I saw it!" I was so excited. My mum didn't believe it. "I've got a video," I shouted. I showed my parents and my brother and sister, but we couldn't see anything. There was nothing – just the loch and the noise of the wind. I couldn't believe it. "But I saw it!" I said. My dad put his arm around me and said, "Never mind, Jaden. I talked to Mum; we're going to come back next year. Maybe for two weeks." As we drove along the lake to Inverness, I looked out of the window at the loch. I still hoped to see Nessie.

A READING

1 Read the text and underline the best title for the story.

1. The black dog
2. Where is Nessie?
3. A holiday in Inverness

2 Read the text again and answer the questions.

1. Where did Jake and his family stay at Loch Ness?

   ____

2. Who doesn't believe in the Loch Ness Monster?

   ____

3. What did the family do at Loch Ness?

   ____

4. Why did Jaden hold his phone all the time?

   ____

5. When did Jaden see the monster?

   ____

6. What did the monster look like?

   ____

7. What happened when Jaden showed the video to his family?

   ____

B WRITING

3 What did Jaden write to his friend? Write his postcard.

C SPEAKING

4 Make a dialogue.

Work with a partner. One of you is student A, the other is student B. Act a dialogue.

Student A

You are on holiday with your family. It's the last day. You want to go to a theme park. Your brother / sister wants to go to a museum. Talk about what to do.

Student B

You are on holiday with your family. It's the last day. You want to go to a museum. Your brother / sister wants to go to a theme park. Talk about what to do.

1 Find a topic for your story.

Write a story or a report for a school magazine. Write about something that happened to you during your last summer holidays. Write notes.

→ Folgende Fragen können dir helfen ein Thema zu finden:

Überlege, was du in den letzten Ferien gemacht hast.
Hast du deinen Freunden oder deiner Familie von einem Erlebnis erzählt?
War es lustig oder interessant für deine Zuhörer?
Wenn dir nichts einfällt, kannst du einfach eine Geschichte erfinden.

____

____

2 Collect information for your story.

Answer the questions.

Who?	
When?	
Where?	
What?	
How?	

3 Make a timeline for your story.

→ Trage die Ereignisse deiner Geschichte in einen Zeitstrahl ein.
So kannst du besser sehen, was wann passiert ist.

4 Collect words for your story in a mind map.

Sammele Wörter, die du für deine Geschichte brauchst. Schreibe alles, was zusammen gehört, unter einen Oberbegriff.
Ergänze diese in deiner Mind map an passender Stelle, so dass du sie später beim Schreiben nicht vergisst.
Schlage Wörter, die du nicht weißt, im Wörterbuch nach.

5 Add adjectives, adverbs and connectives to your mind map.

Adjektive und Adverbien machen deine Geschichte interessanter.

Eine Geschichte klingt besser, wenn man die Sätze miteinander verbindet, z. B. mit and, or, but oder wenn man Sätze mit Wörtern wie first, after that, suddenly, at last einleitet. Benutze nicht zu oft then.
Ergänze deine Mind map an den passenden Stellen, so dass du die Wörter später beim Schreiben nicht vergisst.

6 Make a plan for your story.

Put your ideas from exercises 1–4 in the table. Write notes.

title		It is easier to find a title after you have written the story.
introduction		Use the information from exercise 2 here.
parts of the story		Put everything in one part that goes together. Use your timeline and mind map to help you.
ending		Finish your story. Use words like finally or at last.

7 Write a draft of your story in your exercise book.

Mache zuerst einen Entwurf und schreibe nur in jede zweite Zeile, so dass du Platz für Korrekturen hast. Hake alles, was du verwendet hast, in der Tabelle oben ab. So vergisst du nichts beim Schreiben.
Schreibe deine Geschichte im Simple past.
Verwende, wo nötig, die wörtliche Rede.

8 Check your text. Use the list below.

Rechtschreibung
Hast du alle Wörter richtig geschrieben? Achte besonders auf:

- Buchstaben, die geschrieben, aber nicht gesprochen werden (z. B. walk)
- gleiche Schreibung, aber unterschiedliche Bedeutung (z. B. see ⟷ sea)
- die Verdoppelung der Endkonsonanten (z. B. stop → stopping, stopped, plan → planning, planned)
- ‚y' wird zu ‚ie':
  - in der 3. Person Singular (z. B. carry → he carried, aber buy → she buys)
  - im Plural (z. B. city → cities, aber boy → boys)
  - bei der Steigerung von Adjektiven (z. B. happy → happier, (the) happiest)
- die Wortendung ‚-le' (z. B. simple, title)
- den Apostroph (z. B. she is → she's, Brad's bike, the Browns' house)

Wenn du dir nicht sicher bist, schau hinten in deinem Buch oder in einem Wörterbuch nach.

Groß- und Kleinschreibung
- Hast du jeden Satz mit einem Großbuchstaben begonnen?
- Diese Wörter musst du immer groß schreiben: Monatsnamen (z. B. January), Wochentage (z. B. Monday), Eigennamen (z. B. Tom), geografische Namen (z. B. Greenwich).

Zeichensetzung
- Endet jeder Satz mit einem Punkt? Endet jede Frage mit einem Fragezeichen?
- Denke an die Anführungszeichen bei der wörtlichen Rede.

Grammatik
- Hast du überall die richtige Zeitform verwendet?
- Hast du, wo es nötig ist, die Mehrzahl verwendet?

9 Write a clean copy of your story in your exercise book. Add photos or other pictures.

Unit 4

In Northern Ireland

74/2 ## 1 What can you do in Northern Irleland?

a) Write a sentence for each photo.

1. *You can see* ______________________
2. ______________________

3. ______________________
4. ______________________

b) Choose one of the photos and write four sentences about it in your exercise book.

9
75/3 ## 2 (LISTENING) Listen to the tourist guide and complete the fact card.

Belfast

capital of ______________________

about ____________ inhabitants

built in ______________________

famous for ______________________

murals: ______________________

Belfast today: ______________________

1 Match the sentence parts. Draw lines.

76/1

1. I've moved house and I'm fed	evenings.
2. I can't see my friends any	more.
3. I miss them all so	least.
4. My brothers drive me	crazy.
5. Even when I'm not at school, I'm bored all	up.
6. I sometimes call my friends in the	much.
7. We can write e-mails at	wrong.
8. I don't like it here. My parents were	day.

2 Match the adjectives with the pictures.

77/5a)

scared | smart | naughty | glad | furious | cautious | horrible | positive

1 
______

2 
______

3 
______

4 
______

5 
______

6 
______

7 
______

8 
______

3 Find adjectives for the definitions.

77/5b)

1. When your friends don't invite you to their party, you feel down.
2. When an exercise isn't difficult, it's ______.
3. When you are ill and haven't slept all night, you feel ______.
4. When you think someone is going to buy you a new phone, you feel ______.
5. When you understand something very quickly, you are ______.
6. When you want to be careful and not say too much, you are ______.
7. When you find out that your sister is wearing your favourite T-shirt, you feel ______.
8. When you are very confident, you are ______.

10 77/6

4 (LISTENING) Listen to Julie and her mum. Tick the right box.

	right	wrong	not in the text
1. Sarah moved two months ago.	☐	☐	☐
2. Julie's mum lived in a little village when she was a child.	☐	☐	☐
3. Julie's mum lived in Cornwall.	☐	☐	☐
4. Sarah makes friends easily.	☐	☐	☐
5. Sarah's school is in the village where she lives.	☐	☐	☐
6. Julie wants to invite Sarah for the weekend.	☐	☐	☐
7. There was a German tourist at Sarah's bed and breakfast.	☐	☐	☐
8. Sarah is Julie's best friend.	☐	☐	☐

77/6

5 (WRITING) Do you like living in the city / country? Why / why not? Give your opinion.

I like living in ... because | There is / there are ... | garden / shops / cinema / ... | You can ...

____

____

____

____

____

____

____

____

____

78/8

6 Complete the sentences.

1. If our house *was* (be) bigger, I would invite Sarah to live with us.
2. If Sarah ____________ (live) here in Belfast, she would see her old friends again.
3. Sarah would be happier if she ____________ (go) to her old school again.
4. If we ____________ (see) Sarah's parents, they would agree.
5. We would go shopping every weekend if we ____________ (be) together again.
6. If we ____________ (spend) a lot of time together, we would have arguments too.
7. We would talk about it and be friends again if we ____________ (have) an argument.
8. But if Sarah ____________ (stay) with us, her parents would miss her a lot.

78/8

7 Look at the pictures and complete the sentences.

1 be

2 visit

3 go

4 swim

5 take

6 eat

1. If my best friend moved to Northern Ireland, I would be sad ______ .
2. If she lived in Belfast, I ______ .
3. If I was in Belfast with her, we ______ .
4. If the weather was good, we ______ .
5. If we wanted to go to the Giant's Causeway, her dad ______ .
6. If we found a café there, we ______ .

3/9a)

8 Put in the right verb forms.

Mum: Brad, if you invited ______ (invite) that new boy next door, you ______ (get) to know him a bit.

Brad: Mum, if that boy ______ (be) friendlier, I ______ (ask) him to my birthday party. And if he ______ (smile) sometimes, people ______ (not think) he was so horrible.

Mum: He's just lonely, Brad. If you ______ (have to) move to Belfast, you ______ (feel) like him.

Brad: I ______ (make) new friends easily if we ______ (live) in Belfast.

Mum: Don't be so unfriendly. Look, he's over there!

Brad: Oh, OK. Hey, Ashley! Do you want to come to my birthday party on Saturday?

Ashley: Hi Brad! Thanks! I ______ to come if I ______ already ______ (not make) other plans for the weekend.

Brad: OK, maybe next time.

3/9b)

9 What would you do if…? Write your own sentences.

find some money | meet a famous actor | see a spider | want a new phone

1. If I found ______
2. ______
3. ______
4. ______

79/10

10 What would you do in these situations?

a) Write questions for your partner.

b) Write down your partner's answers.

1. your friend tells stories about you

   What would you do if ______

   Answer: ______

2. go on holiday with your best friend

   Where would you go if ______

   Answer: ______

3 your best friend misses school

   What would you do if ______

   Answer: ______

4. you forget your homework

   What would you tell your teacher if ______

   Answer: ______

c) Write three more questions for your partner in your exercise book and write down his / her answers.

79/11

11 (WRITING) Write an e-mail and give advice to a friend.

a) Read Sarah's e-mail.

E-MAIL

Dear Julie,

I've lost my phone – again!!! Dad will kill me! I'm sure he won't buy me a new phone again, but I need one. What can I do? Please help!

See you,
Sarah.

b) Write an e-mail to Sarah and give her some advice.

bad news | If I were you, I … | Why don't you … | Think positive … | See you

E-MAIL

______

______

______

______

______

______

1 At the shop

80/1 a) What are the words?

1. ______
2. ______
3. ______
4. ______
5. ______
6. ______
7. ______

1/4a) b) Complete the shopping dialogue.

A: Hello, can I ______ ?

B: Yes, ______ four stamps, please.

A: Anything ______ ?

B: Yes, ______ these two postcards, please.

A: ______ £5.85.

B: Here ______ .

A: Thanks, and £4.15 is your ______ .

1/4b) c) Match the situations with the sentences. Draw lines.

1. You want to buy a stamp, but there's nothing in your wallet.
2. The assistant can't change your ten pound note.
3. You don't like the jam they have at the shop.
4. You wanted to buy apples, but they don't look good.
5. The shop has run out of your favourite chocolate.

I've changed my mind.

Do you have another brand?

I don't have any money left.

We can order some for you.

Do you have the exact change?

2 Find the words for the things and write them below.

81/5

a packet of: ______

a jar of: ______

a bottle of: ______

3 (LISTENING) Listen to the dialogue in the shop.

11 81/5

a) Write Dan's shopping list.

b) Listen again and tick the things he could buy.

c) How much change did Dan get? ____________

4 Compare the things.

82/7 a) Look at the picture and complete the sentences.

1. The chocolate cake is _cheaper than_ the strawberry cake. (cheap)
2. The strawberry cake is ______________ the chocolate cake. (big)
3. The chocolate cake is ______________ the scones. (expensive)
4. The strawberry cake is ______________ cake. (big)
5. The scones are ______________ the other cakes. (small)
6. The scones are ______________ cakes. (cheap)

82/8a) b) Look at the picture and use the words to make sentences.

as ... as | more ... than | not as ... as | -er than | less than

1. The bar of dark chocolate is _more expensive than_ the bar of white chocolate. (expensive)
2. The nuts are ______________ the bar of dark chocolate. (expensive)
3. The bar of white chocolate is ______________ the nuts. (expensive)
4. The nuts are ______________ the chocolate. (healthy)
5. The bar of white chocolate is ______________ the bar of dark chocolate. (big)

/8a)

5 Complete the table.

small		
	nicer	
		most beautiful
funny		
	more interesting	
		wettest
spectacular		
		best
bad		

/8a)

6 Put in the right words.

Ballyronan still doesn't feel like home. It's getting better, but I often wake up and hope that I'm in my old bedroom in Belfast. Belfast is bigger than ________ (big) this village and ________ (exciting) too. When I came here, I thought that Ballyronan must be the ________ (boring) place in the whole world. This village is ________ (healthy) Belfast, but I can't believe that I will ever love it here. My new neighbours are just as ________ (friendly) the people in Belfast and they are even ________ (funny) – they make me laugh a lot – but I miss my old friends, especially Julie. She is ________ (good) friend that a person can have. My new friend Alex isn't as ________ (nice) Julie, but he's a good friend too. And maybe one day in the future I'll think he's ________ (interesting) person in the world.

/8b)

7 (WRITING) Compare the two sights in Northern Ireland.

interesting | cheap | spectacular | ...

The Titanic Museum i ________________

____

____

8 Put in some or any.

83/9a)

Assistant: Hello. Can I help you?

Customer: Yes, please. Do you have _any_ brown bread?

Assistant: No, I'm sorry. We don't have ________ brown bread at the moment, but we have ________ very tasty white bread.

Customer: OK. Thanks. I'll have a loaf of white bread, please. And I'd like ________ jam, too.

Assistant: We have ________ raspberry jam but we don't have ________ strawberry jam. Is raspberry jam OK?

Customer: Yes, that's great, thanks. And do you have ________ milk?

Assistant: Well, I don't have ________ milk in the shop, but I have ________ in my kitchen. Wait a minute and I'll get you ________ milk. Would you like one bottle or two?

Customer: Oh no. I don't want to take your milk. Then you won't have ________ milk for your breakfast.

Assistant: Don't worry. We have ________ cows in our garden. We have a big garden!

Customer: Thank you very much.

9 Look at the pictures. Write sentences with some or any.

83/9b)

1 

You can give ________________________________

2 

I'll ________________________________

3 

Oh no! ________________________________

4 

____

5 

____

1 (SPEAKING) A shopping dialogue

3/10

a) Read the role cards.

Partner A
You are the customer.
You want to buy these things:
2 bottles of milk
1 jar of strawberry jam
1 packet of tissues
1 loaf of brown bread
1 jar of peanut butter

Partner B
You are the shop assistant.
Look at the things in the shop.
How much do they cost?
Decide what the tissues and light bulbs cost.
Practise saying the prices first.

b) Act the role play with a partner.

c) Make your own role cards.

Partner A
You are the shop assistant. Write down 4 more things you can sell in your shop. Write down prices for them.

____

____

____

Partner B
You are the customer. Write your own shopping list.

____

____

____

____

d) Act your role play.

85/5

1 (READING) Read the blog entry.

INTERNET

I'm Northern Irish

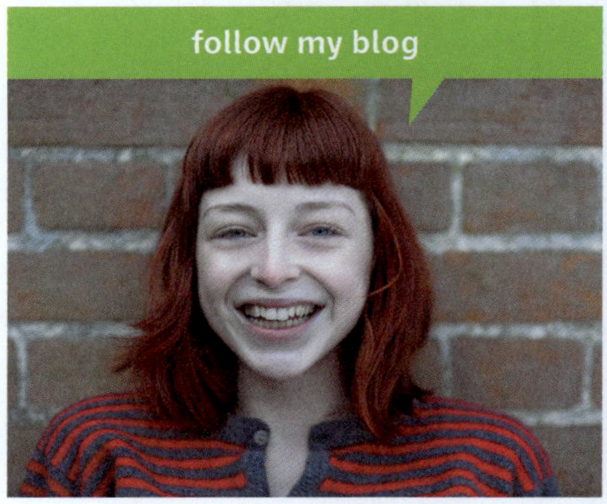

"Are you Irish?"
"No, I'm Northern Irish," I said.
"Yes, so you're Irish – but from the north," said the Italian girl who I met in a youth hostel in London. It's often like this when I meet people who aren't from the British Isles. I usually give up and say yes, but on Saturday I decided to explain things.

"The people who live in Northern Ireland are actually British – we also have the pound and the Queen. In the rest of Ireland the people are Irish and they have the euro like many other countries in Europe. Of course, many Catholics who live in Northern Ireland feel Irish because Northern Ireland is in Ireland, and most of the Protestants feel British. Ah, it's difficult to explain[1] – but my dad is Catholic and my mum is Protestant and I feel Northern Irish."
There were lots of teenagers at the youth hostel from all over the world and they were interested in Northern Ireland. It was great – that meant they were interested in me although I was the youngest. I didn't want to talk about the Troubles – it's the most famous thing about Northern Ireland, but it's not something that most people are proud of. Anyway, the Troubles stopped before I was born. But when I told them that Northern Ireland is very small (fewer people live there than in London), they wanted to know about famous Northern Irish people. And it was then that I told them about Mairead Maguire. They looked at me and asked, "Mairead Maguire?"

"She's not famous," they said.
"Well, she won the Nobel Peace Prize in 1976," I told them. "She's famous." I told them about how it all started – about the accident when three of Maguire's nieces and nephews[2] died in a car accident. It was an accident, but it happened because of the Troubles. A solider shot[3] the driver of a car because he thought the driver was a Catholic terrorist. He died and his car killed the children.

A woman, Betty Williams, saw the accident and was angry. She called for a demonstration of women for peace, and two days later hundreds of women walked through the streets. The women walked past Mairead Maguire's house and she went out and took part in the demonstration. Mairead Maguire and Betty Williams became the leaders of a peace group called, 'The Peace People'. Until then when a Catholic killed a Protestant, a Protestant killed a Catholic and then another Catholic killed a Protestant… You know? Mairead Maguire said that you can't make peace if you kill somebody. They fought for peace with words, but they made a lot of enemies. They were very brave and they really changed how people thought. A few years later Maguire and Williams won the Nobel Peace Prize, but they didn't stop there. They are still fighting for peace in the world now.
"She's more than famous," said a boy. "She's a hero! A Northern Irish hero."

1 explain [ɪk'spleɪn] – *erklären*; 2 nephew ['nefju:] – *Neffe*; 3 shoot [ʃu:t], shot [ʃɒt], shot [ʃɒt] – *(er)schießen*

85/5

2 Find the German word.

1. euro ______
2. Nobel Peace Prize ______
3. terrorist ______
4. demonstration ______

Manche Wörter kannst du dir selbst erschließen. Kennst du schon ein ähnliches Wort auf Englisch? Oder ähnelt es einem deutschen Wort?

85/5

3 Read the text again and choose the right answer.

1. The people who live in Northern Ireland are …
   a) Irish. ☐ b) British. ☐ c) English. ☐
2. The teenagers at the hostel wanted to know about famous Northern Irish …
   a) bands. ☐ b) people. ☐ c) sights. ☐
3. Mairead Maguire won …
   a) a prize for her music. ☐ b) the Nobel Peace Prize. ☐ c) a prize for her recipes. ☐
4. Three of Maguire's nieces and nephews died in …
   a) a car accident. ☐ b) a train accident. ☐ c) a bus accident. ☐
5. Betty Williams called for a …
   a) a doctor. ☐ b) an ambulance. ☐ c) a demonstration. ☐

85/5

4 Answer the questions.

1. Why doesn't the narrator usually talk about the Troubles?
   ______
2. Why was the accident caused by the Troubles?
   ______
   ______
3. Who is Betty Williams? ______
4. What did Betty Williams and Mairead Maguire do?
   ______

85/5

5 (WRITING) Find out more about Betty Williams on the internet and write a short biography of her.

______
______
______
______
______

INTERNET

B & B rules

If you want to stay at a bed and breakfast, there are some general rules you should follow:

- A B & B is normally someone's home. Don't damage anything and don't take anything home with you.
- Respect other guests. Sometimes you can't lock your room. If a door is closed, don't go in.
- Find out what the hours are for checking in, checking out and for breakfast.
- Don't use the B & B phone for personal calls. Use your mobile phone.
- Follow the instructions on reservations. Most B & Bs have websites that explain if you should make reservations online or by phone. If you call the B & B, don't phone during breakfast times because people will be busy making and serving breakfast.
- Ask questions about the place where you are staying. Nobody knows the area better than the owners of a B & B.

86/1

1 (MEDIATION) Lies dir die Regeln durch und beantworte die Fragen.

1. Was bedeutet respektvoller Umgang im B & B?

___

___

2. Wie ist das mit dem Telefonieren?

___

___

3. Was soll man beim Reservieren beachten?

___

___

86/1

2 (MEDIATION) At the B & B

Du bist mit deiner Mutter im Frühstücksraum eines B & B. Vermittle zwischen ihr und der Inhaberin.

Your mum: Ich mag diesen Toast überhaupt nicht. Frag mal, ob es auch Bauernbrot gibt.

You: Excuse me, ___

Woman: Yes, I'll get you some. Would you like anything else?

You: ___

Your mum: Ja, ich hätte gerne Zitrone für den Tee.

You: ___

Woman: I'm sorry, I don't have any lemons. But I can get you some milk.

You: ___

Your mum: Milch? In meinem Tee? Nein danke.

You: ___

Ziel 1: I can understand information about Northern Ireland.

→ ⊙ a3sb38

Northern Ireland – the happiest place in the British Isles!

In 2015 the inhabitants of the British Isles answered questions about their lives and how happy they were. The results showed that the inhabitants of Northern Ireland were happier than anywhere else in the UK and Ireland. Why was that? Many people were surprised. The Troubles in Northern Ireland were a problem for many years. The country was poor; lots of people didn't have a job and over 3,000 people died in the Troubles. "A lot has changed after the end of the Troubles. People are happy that they survived," a woman said. "There have always been lots of problems in Ireland, so when people have enough to eat and are healthy, they are happy." A young man said, "Why shouldn't we be happy? It's a great place to live. We have beautiful countryside – the sea and mountains – lots to do and great people!"

Right or wrong? Tick the right box.

	right	wrong
1. People in Northern Ireland are the happiest in the UK and Ireland.	☐	☐
2. Many people expected that result.	☐	☐
3. During the Troubles many people couldn't find work.	☐	☐
4. Little changed after the end of the Troubles.	☐	☐
5. People are happy when they have enough food and are healthy.	☐	☐
6. Northern Ireland is a great place to live.	☐	☐

6P

→ p. 86/1

Ziel 2: I can give advice to a friend.

→ ⊙ k4c9he → ⊙ p565kd

Write an answer to Harry's e-mail and give him advice.

bad news | don't give up | If I were you … | I'm sure … | Maybe | Be positive | Wait to hear from me!

E-MAIL

Dear Tom,
I'm so fed up. My mum says that I can't go with you all on holiday. She says I have to go with them to Ireland. They're going to travel around and stay in B&Bs. It will be so boring!! What can I do? I want to go camping with you! My mum says we're too young. She knows that we won't be far from your aunt's house, and that we'll have our bikes with us. She says that the roads are too dangerous in Devon and we could have an accident. Please help.
See you, Harry.

5P

→ p. 86/2

Ziel 3: I can buy things and have a conversation in a small shop.

→ ◎ m4cr3d → ◎ x7vd9n

Look at the shopping list and complete the dialogue.

Shopping list

1 jar of raspberry jam
1 jar of peanut butter
1 bottle of milk
2 packets of sliced bread
3 stamps for Europe

Assistant: Hello, ______________________________ ?

You: Yes, I'd ______________________________ .

Assistant: I'm sorry, we don't have any raspberry jam today. Would you like some strawberry jam?

You: Yes, please. And ______________________________ ______________________________ .

Assistant: We have a small jar for £1.80 or a big jar for £3.00.

You: I'd like the big jar, please. And ______________________________ ?

Assistant: Yes, of course. Here ______________________________ .

You: And ______________________________ .

Assistant: I'm sorry, ______________________________ . But we have loaves of white bread.

You: OK, ______________________________ . ______________________________ ?

Assistant: Yes, how many would you like?

You: ______________________________ , please.

Assistant: Here you are. ______________________________ ?

You: No, thanks.

Assistant: OK. ______________________________ £14.50, please.

6P

→ p. 87/3

Ziel 4: I can understand a newspaper report about a disaster.

→ ◎ c74e2b

Read the text on pages 84–85 in your book again and answer the questions.

1. Why did the Titanic sink? ______________________________
2. Why did so many people die? ______________________________
3. Why didn't the Titanic have enough lifeboats? ______________________________
4. Why did a dog save the lives of some passengers? ______________________________
5. Which law is there today to make sure that there are no more accidents like this? ______________________________

5P

→ p. 87/4

Ziel 5: I can pass on information about a B & B.

INTERNET

Loch Neagh B & B

The Loch Neagh is a big, old house 50 metres from the lake itself. We have six rooms which are big enough for families.
Have breakfast in our breakfast room with lovely views of the lake. In the summer you can have breakfast in the garden.

We also have a small boat, which guests can borrow to explore the lake or to go fishing.

In the evenings guests can sit together in the big living room and talk about their day, listen to music or watch TV.

For reservations please fill in the contact form below or call 02894 43489.

a) Lies dir die Webseite durch und beantworte die Fragen.

1. Wo befindet sich das B & B? ______
2. Wie viele Zimmer haben sie? ______
3. Wo kann man frühstücken?
______
4. Was kann man abends machen?
______
5. Was kann man am See machen?
______

b) Du bist mit deiner Familie zu Gast im Loch Neagh B & B. Ein deutscher Tourist möchte ein Zimmer buchen. Vermittle zwischen ihm und der Inhaberin.

Tourist: Hello! Ich würde gerne hier übernachten. Haben Sie ein Zimmer frei?
You: ______
Woman: Yes, we have a room. How long would you like to stay?
You: ______
Tourist: Wir sind nicht ganz sicher. Vielleicht zwei oder drei Nächte.
You: ______
Woman: A room costs £65 per night with breakfast.
You: ______
Tourist: Das klingt gut. Dann hätte ich gerne das Zimmer für zwei Nächte.
You: ______

5P

→p. 87/5

Lösungen online
ap57u5

○ **Ziel 1: I can understand information about Northern Ireland.**

Northern Ireland – a great place for a holiday!

Northern Ireland has a population of less than two million. About 280,000 people live in Belfast. This means that there is a lot of beautiful countryside with a spectacular coast.

You can travel easily from Belfast to the mountains, the coast or the lakes. It is a great place for everyone who loves to be outside.

For those people who prefer being in a big city, there's a lot to do in Belfast. You you can go to museums and theatres. If you like shopping, you'll find lots of great shops in Belfast.

1. About 280,000 people live in ______________________.
2. It has a lot of beautiful countryside with ______________________.
3. You can travel easily from Belfast to ______________________.
4. It is a great place for everyone who ______________________.
5. In Belfast, you can go to ______________________.
6. If you like shopping, you'll find ______________________.

○ **Ziel 2: I can give advice to a friend.**

Complete the e-mail.

Call me later | I have a good idea | Why don't you ask her | Good luck | That sounds awful

E-MAIL

Dear Alicia,
I have a big problem! I really want the black dress we saw in the shop yesterday. It would be great for your birthday party on Saturday, but Mum doesn't want to give me the money. She says I already have enough clothes, which is so unfair because most of them are so old even Grandma wouldn't want to wear them. I really want that dress. What can I do? Please help me!
Lisa

Dear Lisa,

______________________ ! Of course you need a new dress for the party! ______________________ . Emily has lots of cool dresses and she often lends them to her friends.

______________________ ? ______________________ and tell me what she said.

______________________ ! Alica

○ **Ziel 3: I can buy things and have a conversation in a small shop.**

Put the dialogue in the right order.

- ☐ OK. That's £6.59, please.
- ☐ Hello. Can I help you?
- ☐ Oh, I'm sorry. We don't have any raspberry jam. We've got some strawberry jam.
- ☐ Here you are. Would you like a big or a small jar of peanut butter?
- ☐ A small jar, please. Thanks, that's all I need.
- ☐ Then I'll take the strawberry jam. And I'd like some peanut butter too.
- ☐ Yes, I'd like a jar of raspberry jam, please.
- ☐ Here you are. Thank you.

○ **Ziel 4: I can understand a newspaper report about a disaster.**

Read the text on pages 84–85 in your book again and tick the right answers.

1. The Titanic sank because it hit ...	a) an iceberg. ☐	b) another ship. ☐
2. The Titanic didn't have enough ...	a) passengers. ☐	b) lifeboats. ☐
3. The ship's builders were sure that their ship ...	a) was safe. ☐	b) was beautiful. ☐
4. The ship's doctor ...	a) did not survive. ☐	b) survived. ☐
5. A ship found a lifeboat because ...	a) the people shouted. ☐	b) a dog barked. ☐
6. The Titanic Museum has Dr Simpson's last ...	a) letter. ☐	b) photo. ☐

○ **Ziel 5: I can pass on information about a B & B.**

Lies dir die Webseite durch und beantworte die Fragen.

INTERNET

THE B & B | BOOKING | CONTACT

Carnside B & B

- Eleven rooms
- Each room with own bathroom
- Breakfast from 7:00 until 10:00
- Big living room with TV
- free Wi-Fi
- big garden
- 15 minutes' walk to the Giant's Causeway

1. Wieviele Zimmer gibt es? ______
2. Hat jedes Zimmer ein Badezimmer? ______
3. Wann gibt es Frühstück? von ______
4. Gibt es Fernseher auf dem Zimmer? ______
5. Gibt es kostenloses Internet? ______
6. Was kann man dort unternehmen? ______

93/4

1 Look at the picture and answer the questions.

1. What kind of place can you see in the picture? ______
2. Where (which town / country) do you think it is and why?

______

3. Who can you see?

______

4. What can you see?

______

93/4

2 What can you see in the different parts of the picture?

in the foreground / background | on the left / right side | in the middle | at the top / bottom | in the upper / lower corner

______

______

______

______

______

______

______

93/4

3 What are the people doing?

93/4

4 What are the people saying?

a) Choose two people from the picture and write a short dialogue for them.

b) Act your dialogue with a partner.

93/4

5 Talk about the pictures.

a) Choose one of the pictures and describe it to your partner.

b) Which of these places would you like to visit? Why / why not? Talk to your partner.

A LISTENING

12 1 **Listen to the radio news. Which picture is correct?**

12 2 **Listen again and complete the sentences.**

1. The ship was on its way from Liverpool to ______________ .
2. The ship sank near ________________________________ .
3. 58 of the __________ people on board are safe now.
4. The captain of the ship made an emergency call at __________ this morning.
5. Emergency services arrived at the ship ________________ later.
6. Hundreds of people arrived at ______________________ to meet their friends and family.
7. ______________ are looking after anybody who needs help.

13 3 **Listen to the people at the shop. Which of these summaries is correct?**

A Finn goes to a shop to buy a few things when his mum calls him. She tells him that the ship from Liverpool has sunk. Finn worries about his cousins. On his way home he has a car accident. ☐

B Finn goes to a shop to buy a few things. The shop assistant tells him that the ship from Liverpool has sunk. He's worried because his cousins were on the ship. His mum tells him that they missed the ship because of a car accident. ☐

C Finn goes to a shop to buy a few things. He reads in the newspaper that the ship from Liverpool has sunk. Finn is worried because his cousins were on the ship. He tries to call them. ☐

13 4 **Listen again and tick the right box.**

	right	wrong
1. The shop assistant knows Finn.	☐	☐
2. Finn would like six eggs, a raspberry cake and a newspaper.	☐	☐
3. Finn often buys cakes at the shop.	☐	☐
4. Finn has already heard about the disaster.	☐	☐
5. Finn is very white because he's shocked.	☐	☐
6. Finn believes that his cousins were on the ship.	☐	☐
7. Finn's cousins were on the ship, but they are safe now.	☐	☐
8. Finn's cousins are OK.	☐	☐

B WRITING

5 Complete the form with information about yourself.

REGISTRATION FORM

FIRST NAME: ______________________
LAST NAME: ______________________
AGE: ______________________
ADDRESS: ______________________
____
PARENTS: ______________________
BROTHERS / SISTERS: ______________________
____

PETS: ______________________
FAVOURITE SUBJECT(S): ______________________
____
FAVOURITE SPORTS: ______________________
FREE-TIME ACTIVITIES: ______________________
____
FAVOURITE FOOD: ______________________
FAVOURITE FILM: ______________________

6 Write an e-mail to your new friend in Northern Ireland.

Use the information from exercise 5 and write an e-mail to your new friend. Write about 100 words.

Unit 5

Welcome to Ireland

94/2 **1 What's popular in Ireland?**

a) Find a title for each photo.

1. ______________________

2. ______________________

3. ______________________

4. ______________________

b) Choose a photo and write three sentences about it in your exercise book.

94/2 **2 (WRITING) Describe the photo.**

This is a photo of ______________________

____

____

____

____

____

____

96/1

1 What does Conor say about breakfast at his house? Put in the words.

shelf | fridge | prepare | sweet | traditional | cereal | weekdays | help

Breakfast is my favourite meal because I love ______________ . It's so ______________ and so easy to make. Just get the packet from the ______________ , then open the ______________ to get the milk out. We don't have breakfast together on ______________ . But on Saturdays we all eat together and ______________ ourselves to our food. On Sundays we always have a ______________ breakfast. I really like eggs and sausages and sometimes I ______________ them.

97/4

2 What did Leo pack in his trolley suitcase? Write the words.

1. ______________
2. ______________
3. ______________
4. ______________
5. ______________

6. ______________
7. ______________
8. ______________
9. ______________
10. ______________

7/5a)

3 Find the words for the definitions.

1. This is usually white and you need it when you clean your teeth: t______________
2. You use this when your hair is wet: h______________
3. To cut your nails, you need: n______________
4. You need these two things in the shower: s______________ and s______________
5. You need this when your body is wet: t______________
6. You often put this on your body after a shower: b______________
7. You use this when your hair is a mess: c______________

7/5b)

4 Complete the poem.

hair gel | perfume | hairbrush | mirror | soap

I look in the ______________ and see myself.
I've tidied my hair then put the ______________ on the shelf.
I've got some nice ______________
which smells of flowers, I hope.
I'm using my ______________ because I want to smell good.
Would you use some ______________ ? Well, I would!

97/6
14

5 (LISTENING) Listen to Conor and Maddy.

a) What does Maddy want to pack in her bag? Tick the right boxes.

b) Answer the questions.

1. Why is Maddy so excited? ______________________
2. Why does she take two skirts with her? ______________________
3. What does she want to wear when they visit a town? ______________________
4. What are they going to do in the evenings? ______________________
5. Why won't she need a hairdryer? ______________________
6. What does Conor think about shoes? ______________________

6 Complete the dialogue. Use the present progressive.

98/7

Mum: Conor! What _are_ you _doing_ (do) in the kitchen?

Conor: Nothing! I ______________ (drink) some water right now.

Mum: I hope you ______________ (not eat) the chocolate. I need that to make a cake.

Conor: No, Mum. I ______________ (not eat) anything.

Mum: What ________ Leo ________ (do)?

Conor: He's in the garden with Dad. I think they ______________ (play) football.

Mum: Oh, I hope they ______________ (not run) on my new strawberry plants.

Conor: I'll go and see, Mum.

Mum: So what ________ they ________ (do), Conor?

Conor: Don't worry. They ______________ (not play) football.

Mum: Good.

Conor: They ______________ (eat) the chocolate.

98/7

7 Find the signal words for the simple present and the present progressive.

Mark the signal words for the simple present in blue and the words for the present progressive in red.

never	every....	usually	now
often	at the moment	always	sometimes

98/7

8 Simple present or present progressive?

a) Put in the right forms.

1. It's 8 o'clock and Conor gets up. But everything is different today. His parents usually have ______ (have) breakfast at 8 o'clock, but now they ______ (sleep).
2. His sister always ______ (leave) the house at 8 o'clock, but at the moment she ______ (clean) her teeth.
3. The cat usually ______ (catch) mice, but now she ______ (sleep) on the sofa.

4. The neighbours usually ______ (buy) a newspaper, but now they ______ (sit) in the kitchen.
5. The dog always ______ (eat) his dog food, but at the moment he ______ (run) around.
6. The birds usually ______ (make) a noise, but now they ______ (fly) around.

b) Look at the picture. Why is everything different today? ______

8/8a)

9 Simple present or present progressive? Complete the dialogue.

Leo: What are ______ you doing ______ (do) there? What language is that?

Conor: Oh, this is Irish. I ______ (do) my Irish homework right now.

Leo: ______ everyone ______ (learn) Irish at school?

Conor: Yes, children usually ______ (learn) Irish when they start school.

Leo: ______ many people ______ (speak) Irish at home?

Conor: No, we ______ usually ______ (not speak) Irish at home. But we sometimes ______ (watch) Irish TV. I think my grandparents ______ (watch) Irish TV programmes right now. They always ______ (watch) the news in Irish, and they ______ (like) programmes about gardens too. Would you like to learn some Irish, Leo?

Leo: Yes, I'd love to.

10 Simple present or present progressive? Complete the sentences.

98/8b)

CHAT

HairQueen: Hey Linda. What _are you doing_ ______ (do) at the moment?

LaLinda: Hi Maddy. ______ (do) my homework. ______ (always / do) it in the afternoon. ______ (you / do)?

HairQueen: ______ (work) on my blog. ______ (put) in some new photos.

LaLinda: Great! ______ (like) the boy from Germany? ______ (be) his name again?

HairQueen: Leo. He ______ (be) nice.

LaLinda: He ______ (look) good, doesn't he? ☺

HairQueen: He looks OK. ______ (be / too young) for you anyway. ______ (want) to come over for dinner?

LaLinda: No, ______ (still / do) my homework. ☹ See you tomorrow!

11 Whose is it?

99/9a)

a) Put in the right possessive pronouns.

1. Is this Maddy's shampoo? – Yes, it's _hers_ .
2. Don't use my toothbrush! – It's ______ .
3. Have you seen Leo? – I think this bag is ______ .
4. Is this the neighbours' dog? – No, it's not ______ .
5. I think I've found your book. – Is this one ______ ?
6. We live in this house. – It's ______ .

99/9b)

b) Write questions and answers with possessive pronouns.

1. your towel? • yes _Is this_ ______
2. your friends' bikes? • yes ______
3. Conor's bike • no ______

12 Write a dialogue.

99/10

go to the cinema / shopping / ... | do homework / tidy room / ... | on Saturday(s) / ...

A: Hey, let's _go to_ ______ !

B: I'm sorry, I don't have time.

I ______ right now.

A: Oh, too bad. Why don't you do that tomorrow?

B: I always ______ .

100/1

1 Put in the right words.

journey | drumming | traffic | public transport | moves
homepage | perform | helpful | dances | rhythm

It's easy to get around in Dublin. You can use ______________ ______________. Of course, you can drive too. There's a lot of ______________ in Dublin so leave enough time for your ______________. You can find ______________ information on our ______________.

Irish ______________ are very popular, and Irish ______________ music is too. There are many dance groups which ______________ Irish dances. If you like the ______________, you will learn some simple ______________ at a dance workshop.

1/3a)

2 Find the words for the definitions.

1. not early or late: ______________
2. use one to find a street: ______________
3. get off one train and get on another: ______________
4. you pay this when you get on a bus: ______________
5. an old ticket isn't this any more: ______________
6. like a train but runs on a road: ______________
7. go here to get on a train: ______________
8. wait here for a bus: ______________

1/3b)

3 Find the words for public transport.

____
____
____
____
____
____
____
____
____

D	F	R	E	T	U	R	N	T	I	C	K	E	T
B	F	J	S	H	J	W	F	B	D	T	K	D	G
U	C	V	Q	Y	C	P	O	J	I	W	E	E	F
S	F	B	W	D	V	O	G	H	W	G	M	Z	E
F	J	D	E	A	B	I	N	F	E	H	O	F	G
J	Z	R	R	I	N	Z	V	D	E	V	N	U	U
S	I	N	G	L	E	T	I	C	K	E	T	H	K
F	A	D	G	Y	S	H	U	I	L	C	H	R	B
K	T	U	I	R	Z	L	R	I	Y	D	L	R	D
R	U	Z	T	M	M	T	C	D	H	O	Y	T	U
B	A	N	N	U	A	L	X	S	K	I	S	W	F
K	L	K	H	G	F	D	S	I	E	Q	R	J	J
T	R	A	V	E	L	E	Y	A	T	R	A	I	N

15 101/4

4 (LISTENING) Listen to Conor and Leo.

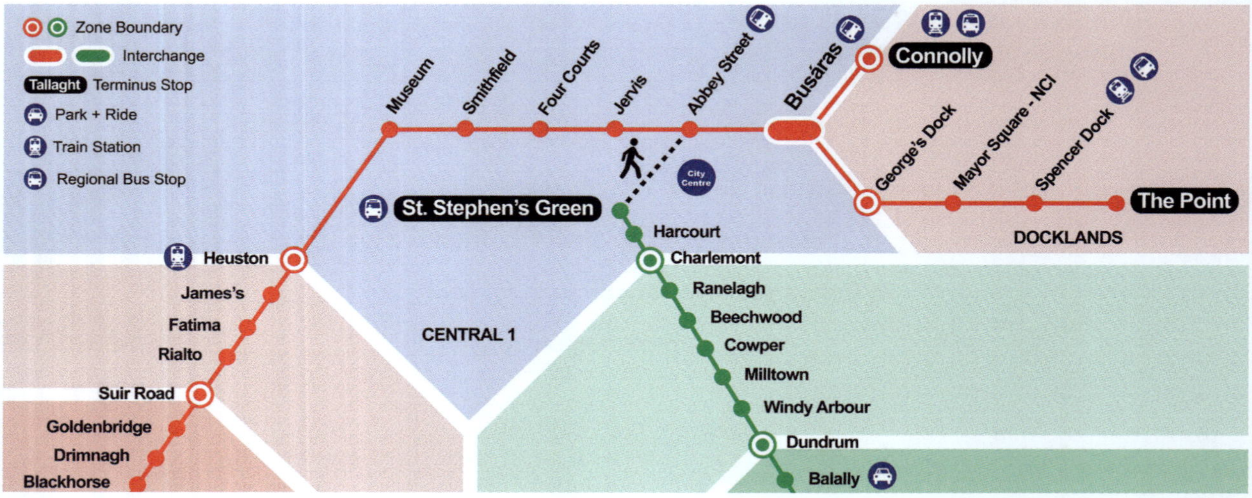

a) Where is Leo? Draw an ✕ on the map.

b) Draw Leo's journey on the map.

c) Complete the sentences.

1. Conor is …

a) at a concert. ☐	b) at a friend's house. ☐	c) at the museum. ☐

2. Leo can get to Conor …

a) by train. ☐	b) by tram. ☐	c) by bus. ☐

3. The Museum stop is …

a) two minutes away. ☐	b) five minutes away. ☐	c) ten minutes away. ☐

4. Somebody will show Leo …

a) the tram. ☐	b) a map. ☐	c) the way. ☐

5. Conor will meet Leo …

a) at his friend's house. ☐	b) at the Beechwood stop. ☐	c) at the St. Stephen's Green stop. ☐

102/6

5 What can or mustn't you do in Ireland? Complete the sentences.

1. Cars drive on the left. You mustn't drive on the right.
2. Pubs are for adults. Children ______________ go into a pub without their parents.
3. The Republic of Ireland is in the European Union. You ______________ use euros.
4. Public transport is very good in Dublin. But you ______________ use it without a ticket.
5. The Irish love music. You ______________ go to a lot of concerts.
6. There are lots of art programmes. You ______________ learn how to dance and make films.
7. People are very friendly. But you ______________ forget to be polite.
8. On St Patrick's Day you ______________ watch a lot of parades.

6 What must or mustn't the students do?

2/7a) a) Complete the sentences.

1. The students _must_ ______ do their homework on time.
2. The students ______ run in the corridors.
3. Conor ______ go to his saxophone lessons on Tuesdays.
4. Teachers ______ give too much homework.
5. Students ______ talk when the teacher is talking.
6. Teachers ______ correct the students' homework every week.

2/7b) b) Write three rules for your school.

1. ______
2. ______
3. ______

7 What must Conor do before Leo arrives? What needn't he do? Look at the list and write sentences.

103/8

1. _Conor must wash the car._
2. _He needn't_ ______
3. _He_ ______
4. ______
5. ______
6. ______
7. ______
8. ______

To do
wash the car – Conor
do the shopping – Mum
prepare dinner – Jamie and Mum
tidy up the living room – Conor
clean the floor – Jamie
feed the cat – Maddy
hang a welcome poster – Conor
make a cake – Conor and Maddy

8 Flying rules. Match the sentences and put in must, mustn't or needn't.

03/9a)

1. Get to the airport early.	You ______ bring anything to drink with you.
2. Buy a ticket.	You ______ sit all the time when the plane is flying.
3. Don't open the window.	You ______ use your mobile.
4. You can walk around.	You ______ open the window.
5. Don't use your mobile.	You _must_ ______ get to the airport early.
6. You can get drinks on the plane.	You ______ buy a ticket before you get on the plane.

9 Put in must, mustn't or needn't.

103/9a)

E-MAIL

Hi Conor,

I had a great time in Ireland and I'm really happy that you're coming to Germany! We'll meet you at the airport and Dad says that you ____________ wait at the 'Treffpunkt', so that we can find you there. Don't worry about your German. You ______________ speak German all the time because my parents speak English too. You know that we live in a flat so we ______________ make too much noise when you're here, but lots of children live here, so we ______________ be too quiet. The weather will be good next week, so you ____________ bring everything you need to go swimming, but you ______________ bring a towel – we have lots here. Well, I ______________ spend too long on this e-mail – I ____________ do my homework.

See you soon, Leo

10 Look at the advert and put in can, mustn't, must or needn't.

103/9b)

Do you love dancing? Yes? Then you ____________ come and try one of our workshops. You ______________ be a good dancer already. We have classes for people who haven't danced before. You will love it. Why don't you come and find out? You ____________ pay for a course at the start. You __________ try a lesson first. You've tried it and think it's too difficult? You ______________ think that – everyone __________ learn it! Do you love music, but you don't want to dance? Then come and try our drumming workshops. We have weekend workshops or workshops during the week. You ______________ bring anything – you __________ use everything in our classrooms.

11 (WRITING) Write rules for visitors to your home.

103/9b)

What must they do? What mustn't they do? What can they do if they ask first?

____

____

____

____

____

____

____

03/10

1 (SPEAKING) Where would you like to go?

a) You are in Dublin with your class and you can spend a Saturday afternoon with your friend. Look at the leaflet. Where would you like to go? Why? Talk to your partner and decide where you want to go together.

The National Museum of Ireland

open: Tuesday–Saturday 10 a.m–5 p.m.
Sunday 2 a.m.–5.p.m.
free for adults and children
tram stop: Museum

Dublin Zoo

open: every day from 9:30 a.m.
adults €16.80, children €12.00
tram stop: Heuston

Peacock Green Café

open: Monday–Friday 7:30 a.m.–5 p.m.
tram stop: Harcourt

Stephen's Green Shopping Centre

open: Monday–Sunday 9 a.m.–7 p.m.
tram stop: St Stephen's Green

b) It's Saturday afternoon and you are at the tram station in Drimnagh. This is where your youth hostel is. Do a role play with your partner and give him / her directions to the places in a). Take turns.

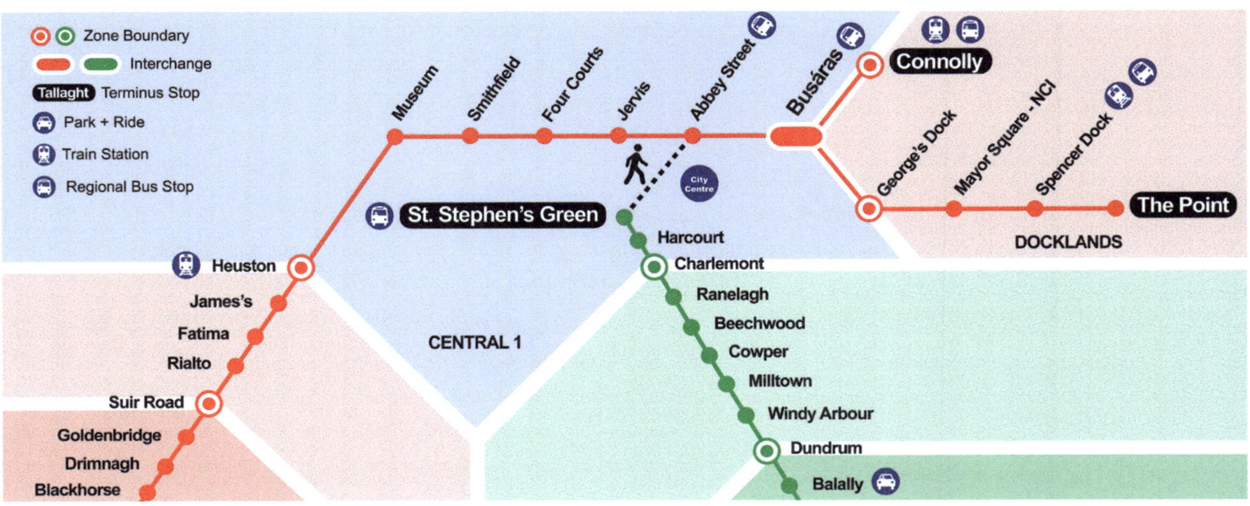

Excuse me | How can we get to ... | Take the ... | Get off | Change | It's ... stops

c) Choose more places from the map and give directions.

1 (READING) Read the entries from Julia's diary.

105/6

10th May

"Oh no!"

That was the only thing I could think of to say when my parents told me that we were going to move to Ireland for a year. My dad is Irish and they met in Dublin when they were both 18. They are proud of their Irish accents, and they go to St Patrick's Day parties here in Stuttgart every year.

"But it always rains in Ireland," I said.

"Yes, but only once a day," answered my dad.

"From morning till night," joked my mum.

"Why can't we go to live in Barcelona or Rome or somewhere where it's always sunny and we can swim in the sea every day?"

"You'll love Ireland," said my dad.

"Julia, we asked you if you wanted to live there for a year," added mum. "You said it was OK with you."

27th August

Guess what! It's raining again. We live in Galway now. It's on the west coast of Ireland and it is, of course, one of the wettest places in the country. We live in a small house near the sea. It would be beautiful if the sun ever came out, but now it's just grey – grey sea, grey sky, grey … Well actually the houses aren't grey. They're all lovely colours – green, red, blue. The houses are lovely – on the outside. On the inside our house is really small and the wind comes in – there is even a draught when the windows are closed! My parents don't seem to notice the weather! They're happy all the time and they drive me crazy. I think I'd feel better if they had one of their big arguments and then we could all be miserable together.

2 Guess the German word.

105/6

1. accent (line 5) ____________________
2. till (line 8) ____________________
3. if (line 12) ____________________
4. draught (line 20) ____________________

3 Choose the right answer.

105/6

1. Julia comes from …
   a) Dublin. ☐
   b) Stuttgart. ☐
2. Julia's parents met in …
   a) Ireland. ☐
   b) Germany. ☐
3. Julia doesn't like …
   a) the rain. ☐
   b) St Patrick's Day parties. ☐
4. At the end of August the weather was …
   a) sunny. ☐
   b) wet. ☐
5. Julia isn't happy because she …
   a) doesn't like her school. ☐
   b) her parents are strict. ☐
6. At the end of the year Julia …
   a) is quite happy in Ireland. ☐
   b) wants to go back to Germany. ☐

5th September

I started my new school on 1st September and I hate it already. It's so difficult to understand the teachers and the other kids. They ask me a question and I look at them and I want to say, "Can you say that again in English?" I know they are speaking English, but it just sounds different when they say it. Other things that I hate are:

- I have to wear a school uniform. I feel like a little kid when I'm wearing it and it doesn't suit me.
- I have to learn Irish. Why? All the kids here learn Irish, but why do I have to?
- All my friends at home in Germany are still on holiday. It's hot there and they go to the swimming pool every day and I'm here and it's raining!!!

24th December

It's almost Christmas. We're going to a party tonight at a friend's house. They're really funny actually. They have two children and they seem to find something funny in everything. My dad says it's because of the weather. If they didn't find things to laugh at, the weather would drive them all crazy! I think he's right. This is our fifth Christmas party already and there's another one tomorrow. I'm quite excited actually, but don't tell my parents! I don't want them to know that I'm quite enjoying it now. I still hate the school uniform though.

26th December

Some friends arrived today from Germany. They're going to spend New Year with us. It's really nice to see them. I couldn't wait to show them our house and the town.
"We don't want to go to town now though, do we?" said Elias. "It's raining."
"Is it?" I asked. I looked out of the window and couldn't believe it. I didn't even notice it.

4 Where can you find the information in the text? Write the line numbers.

105/6

1. Julia's family aren't going to live in Ireland forever. __________
2. Julia doesn't want to move to Ireland. __________
3. Julia thinks the houses in Germany are better. __________
4. Julia's parents sometimes had arguments in Germany. __________
5. At first, Julia finds it difficult to understand the people in Ireland. __________
6. Julia enjoys the Christmas parties. __________

5 (WRITING) Write a diary entry.

105/6

a) On 31st July of the following year, Julia and her family are going to move back to Germany. Write Julia's diary entry for 24th July in your exercise book. Write notes first. The following questions can help you:

1. Is Julia happy in Ireland?
2. Has she made new friends in Ireland?
3. What did she do during the last few months?
4. How does she feel about life in Germany now?

b) Write the diary entry in your exercise book.

Iren in Deutschland

Ungefähr zweitausend Menschen aus Irland wohnen in Hamburg. Die meisten sind junge Menschen, die hier Arbeit gefunden haben. „In Irland ist es gerade sehr schwierig, Arbeit zu finden. Also sind wir nach Hamburg gekommen und wir finden es toll. Die Leute hier sind so offen, freundlich und hilfsbereit, dass ich für immer hier bleiben würde, wenn es nicht so oft regnen würde", sagt Michelle O'Donnell aus Dublin. „Wir vermissen nichts", sagt Patrick Smyth. „Es gibt hier neun irische Kneipen und wir können sogar St Patrick's Day feiern".

Über 500 irische Kinder wohnen hier in Hamburg mit ihren Eltern. „Ich wohne hier, seit ich fünf war, und kann gut Deutsch", sagt Ciara. Dieses Jahr fährt sie mit ihren Eltern zum St Patrick's Day nach München. „Dort gibt es einen Umzug und wir tragen alle grüne Kleidung".

106/1

1 (MEDIATION) Read the text and answer your Irish friend's questions.

1. What does it say about two thousand people from Ireland?
   ____
2. Why do they all live there? ______________________________
3. Do they like it there? ______________________________
4. Why do they like it there? ______________________________
5. What does Patrick Smyth say about St Patrick's Day?
   ____
6. Do Irish children live in Hamburg too?
   ____

106/1

2 (MEDIATION) At Hamburg airport

Du bist am Hamburger Flughafen. Ein Mädchen aus Irland ist gerade angekommen und möchte jetzt ins Stadtzentrum fahren. Vermittle zwischen ihr und dem Mann am Informationsschalter.

Girl: Excuse me. How can I get to the city centre?

You: ______________________________

Man: Sie muss mit der S1 Richtung Wedel fahren und am Hauptbahnhof aussteigen.

You: ______________________________

Girl: Thank you. Where can I buy a ticket, please?

You: ______________________________

Man: Da drüben ist ein Ticketautomat.

You: ______________________________

Girl: Thank you!

Ziel 1: I can understand information about Ireland.

→ ⦾ 7dy84c

A country with two languages

One of the first things that people notice when they go to Ireland are the road signs, which are in English and Irish. In the Republic of Ireland all information must be in English and Irish.

For two thousand years most people who lived in Ireland spoke Irish. But then in the 16th century England invaded Ireland and from that time on more and more people spoke English. From the 19th century most people spoke English as their first language. Today all school children must learn Irish and many schools give some lessons in Irish and some in English. For this reason most people in Ireland can speak Irish. However, only about 10 % of Irish people speak Irish at home. Most of these people live in the west of Ireland. Today people want to protect the Irish language because they understand that a language is an important part of people's lives. There are Irish programmes on TV and Irish is one of the languages which they use in the European Union.

Read the text and answer the questions.

1. Where do most people see Irish first when they visit the country? ______
2. Why did people start to speak English in Ireland? ______
3. When did English become the first language in Ireland?

   ______
4. Where do most Irish people learn to speak Irish? ______
5. Why do people want to protect the Irish language?

   ______

5P
→p. 108/1

Ziel 2: I can talk to people in a host family.

→ ⦾ 6xh4jx → ⦾ 2j5si6

You are in a host family in Ireland and have a few questions. Complete the dialogue.

- need adaptor
- for phone
- borrow?
- forget toothbrush
- buy one somewhere?
- where bathroom?

Mum: Here's your bedroom. Do you have everything you need?

You: ______

______

Mum: Yes, of course. Here you are. Do you need anything else?

You: ______

______

Mum: Yes, there's a supermarket near here. Conor will show you the way.

You: ______

Mum: The bathroom is the first door on the right. The blue towels are for you.

You: ______

Mum: You're welcome.

6P
→p. 108/2

5 Checkpoint

Ziel 3: I can plan a journey by public transport.

→ ⊚ w5fv99 → ⊚ iz53ck

Look at the map. You are at Heuston. Give directions.

1. Tourist 1: Excuse me. How can I get to Connolly?

   You: ______________________________

   ____

2. Tourist 2: Excuse me. How can I get to Cowper?

   You: ______________________________

   ____

4P

→ p. 108/3

Ziel 4: I can understand a story about moving to another country.

→ ⊚ x7v5g7

Read the text on pages 104 and 105 in your book again. What happened first? What happened next? Put the sentences in the right order.

- ☐ When he came home from work, Niamh's dad tried to cheer her up with a poem.
- ☐ Niamh went to her first Paddy's Day party in England.
- ☐ He found a job in England and they moved to Northampton.
- ☐ The three netball girls were at the door, all dressed in green clothes.
- ☐ The factory closed and he couldn't find another job in the area.
- ☐ The netball girls, Sonja, Billy and Nisha didn't answer her calls.
- ☐ Niamh's Dad worked in a factory in Donegal.
- ☐ Niamh thought that nothing could cheer her up.
- ☐ Niamh rushed into her room and grabbed her Paddy's Day outfit.
- ☐ Niamh couldn't help but laugh.
- ☐ It was St Patrick's Day and Niamh felt lonely.
- ☐ The doorbell rang and her dad sent her to open the door.

4P

→ p. 109/4

Ziel 5: I can pass on information about an actor.

Domhnall Gleeson

Domhnall Gleeson ist ein Schauspieler aus Irland, der auch als Schriftsteller und Regisseur tätig ist. Man kennt ihn vor allem in seiner Rolle als Bill Weasley, die er in der siebten und achten Verfilmung der „Harry Potter“-Reihe spielt. Domhnall Gleeson ist der älteste von vier Söhnen des Schauspielers Brendan Gleeson und dessen Frau Mary Gleeson. Er wurde in Dublin geboren und ging dort zur Schule. Nach seinem Studium begann er als Regisseur und Drehbuchautor von Kurzfilmen zu arbeiten. Einen seiner ersten Auftritte vor der Kamera hatte Domhnall 2006 im Film „Studs“, in dem er gemeinsam mit seinem Vater spielte. Danach spielte er in der irischen Fernsehserie „The Last Furlong“ mit.

Zwischen 2007 und 2008 spielte Domhnall Gleeson vor allem am Theater. Anfang 2009 vermittelte ihm sein Vater die Rolle des Bill Weasley in den beiden Teilen von „Harry Potter und die Heiligtümer des Todes“. Sein Vater spielte in den Harry Potter-Filmen die Rolle des Alastor ‚Mad-Eye Moody‘. Domhnall Gleeson zögerte zuerst, weil er keine Rolle annehmen wollte, die er nur seinem Vater zu verdanken hatte. Er änderte dann aber seine Meinung.

Domhnall wurde schon für mehrere Preise nominiert, z. B. den Tony Award, die Irish Film and Television Awards und die British Independent Film Awards. 2011 gewann er beim Internationalen Filmfestival in Berlin einen Preis als bester internationaler Schauspieler.

In „Star Wars: Das Erwachen der Macht“ spielt Domhnall Gleeson die Rolle des General Hux.

Lies den Text und beantworte die Fragen auf Englisch.

1. Where was Domhnall Gleeson born? ____________________
2. Where did he go to school? ____________________
3. Who is his father? ____________________
4. Does he have any brothers or sisters? ____________________
5. What was the title of the first film he acted in? ____________________
6. Why didn't he want to act in the Harry Potter films at first? ____________________

   ____
7. Which role does he play in Star Wars? ____________________

7P

→ p. 109/5

Lösungen online
5gn2qw

○ Ziel 1: I can understand information about Ireland.

The green republic

The Republic of Ireland is in the European Union and it uses the euro. The capital of Ireland is Dublin. Dublin is a very interesting city with lots of art programmes for young people. There are many workshops where you can learn how to dance, act or make films. Music is also very important for Irish people. There are many famous Irish rock and pop bands and many cities have a youth orchestra. People even play music in pubs. The most famous holiday in Ireland is St Patrick's Day.

Every year on 17th March there are parades and parties and most people wear green, the Irish colour.

Read the text and complete the sentences.

1. The Republic of Ireland is in ____.
2. The capital of Ireland is ____.
3. There are many workshops where you can learn how to ____________________.
4. Music is also ____.
5. Every year on St Patrick's day there are ____________________________.

○ Ziel 2: I can talk to people in a host family.

Match the questions and answers.

What would you like for breakfast?	The bathroom is the first door on the right.
Can I borrow your adaptor, please?	I'd like some jam and toast, please.
I've forgotten my shampoo.	Yes, of course. Here you are.
Where is the bathroom, please?	No problem, you can use our shampoo.

○ Ziel 3: I can plan a journey by public transport.

You are at Dundrum station. Look at the map and complete the dialogue.

Tourist: Excuse me. How can I ______________ Spencer Dock?

You: __________________________ to St Stephen's Green. ______________ Abbey Street station. Then ___________________________________ to Spencer Dock.

○ **Ziel 4: I can understand a story about moving to another country.**

Read the text on page 104 and 105 again and tick the right box.

	right	wrong	not in the text
1. Niamh and her dad moved to England two months ago.	☐	☐	☐
2. Niamh doesn't miss her friends and her home in Ireland.	☐	☐	☐
3. Niamh's mum stayed in Ireland.	☐	☐	☐
4. Niamh's dad couldn't find a job in Ireland.	☐	☐	☐
5. Niamh thinks St Patrick's Day is boring.	☐	☐	☐
6. Niamh's dad never goes to the parades on St Patrick's Day.	☐	☐	☐
7. Niamh was homesick.	☐	☐	☐
8. Her new friends take her to a St Patrick's Day party.	☐	☐	☐

○ **Ziel 5: I can pass on information about an actor.**

Saoirse Ronan

Die Schauspielerin Saoirse Ronan wurde 1994 in New York City geboren. Im Alter von drei Jahren zog sie mit ihrer Familie nach Irland und wuchs dort auf. Ihr Vater ist der irische Schauspieler Paul Ronan.
Ihren ersten Auftritt vor der Kamera hatte sie in der irischen Fernsehserie „The Clinic". Seitdem hat sie in einigen bekannten Filmen mitgespielt, z. B. „Wer ist Hanna?" und „Grand Budapest Hotel". 2008 war sie für ihre Rolle in „Abbitte" für den Oscar nominiert, hat ihn aber nicht gewonnen.

Read the text and complete the table.

Saoirse Ronan	
born in	
grew up in	
father	
first TV series	
other films she has acted in	

113/2

1 Write a story about Max's dog.

Read the story on page 112 in your book again. The story starts after Max's dog has died. Write an adventure Max had with his dog before he died.

a) Collect ideas about the dog in a mind map. The following questions can help you:

What was the dog's name?
What kind of dog was it?
What did the dog like to eat?
Did the dog sleep in Max's bed?
What did the dog like to do?

b) Plan your story. Complete the table.

Who is in the story?	
Where does the story take place?	
What happens in your story?	

c) What happens first in your story? What happens next? Make a timeline.

d) Write a draft of your story. Use the simple past.

e) Use the checklist on page 69 in your workbook to check your text.

f) Write a clean copy in your exercise book.

G2 Mit **G** sind die Grammatikkapitel gekennzeichnet und der Reihe nach durchnummeriert.

G1 **Language tip:** Die Seiten kennzeichnen zusätzliche Grammatikkapitel. Du kannst dir die neuen Formen dort wie neue Vokabeln merken oder – wenn du es genau wissen willst – ein paar Regeln dazu lernen.

G1 + G2 Diese Grammatikkapitel findest du im Orange Line 1 Workbook.

G5 + G8 Diese Grammatikkapitel findest du im Orange Line 2 Workbook.

G3 Language tip: Reflexivpronomen und each other

Reflexive pronouns and each other

I have hurt myself.

Ich habe mich verletzt.

Im Englischen werden die Reflexivpronomen mit -self oder -selves gebildet. Im Deutschen werden sie meist mit „mir“ oder „mich“, „dir“ oder „dich“, „sich“ usw. übersetzt.

I bought **myself** a new T-shirt.	Ich habe mir ein neues T-Shirt gekauft.
Can you make **yourself** dinner tonight?	Kannst du dir heute Abend etwas zu essen machen?
He cut **himself** with a knife.	Er hat sich mit einem Messer geschnitten.
She asked **herself** why it happened.	Sie fragte sich, warum es passiert ist.
The cat hurt **itself**.	Die Katze hat sich verletzt.
We enjoyed **ourselves** very much.	Wir amüsierten uns sehr.
Help **yourselves**!	Bedient euch!
They hurt **themselves** in the accident.	Sie haben sich bei dem Unfall verletzt.

Achtung: Beachte den Unterschied zwischen **themselves** und **each other**.

Ben and his sister are looking at **themselves**.	Ben und seine Schwester schauen sich an (= jeder sich selbst).
Ben and his sister are looking at **each other**. (= Ben looks at his sister and she looks at him.)	Ben und seine Schwester schauen sich gegenseitig an (= jeder den anderen).

G4 Adjektive und Adverbien
Adjectives and adverbs

Ein **Adjektiv** (Eigenschaftswort) beschreibt eine Person oder eine Sache.

Beth is a **good** student.	Beth ist eine gute Schülerin.
Climbing is a **dangerous** sport.	Klettern ist ein gefährlicher Sport.

Ein **Adverb** beschreibt, wie jemand etwas tut oder wie etwas geschieht. Im Englischen erkennt man Adverbien durch ein angehängtes **-ly**.

He ran **slowly**.	Er rannte langsam.
It happened **quickly**.	Es geschah schnell.

Achtung Schreibweise: easy → eas**ily**; careful → careful**ly**

Es gibt aber auch unregelmäßige Adverbien:

That's a **good** song.	(Adjektiv)	Das ist ein gutes Lied.
She can sing **well**.	(Adverb)	Sie kann gut singen.

Manche Adverbien verändern sich nicht:

Rugby is a **fast** game.	(Adjektiv)	Rugby ist ein schnelles Spiel.
Look, the players are running **fast**.	(Adverb)	Schau, die Spieler rennen schnell.
This was a **hard** exercise.	(Adjektiv)	Das war eine schwierige Übung.
Mum works **hard** every day.	(Adverb)	Mama arbeitet jeden Tag schwer.

G5 Das Perfekt
Die Grammatikkapitel zum Perfekt findest du im Orange Line 2 Workbook.

G6 Relativsätze mit Relativpronomen
Relative clauses with relative pronouns

Wenn du eine Person oder eine Sache genauer beschreiben willst, verwendest du die Relativpronomen **who**, **which** oder **that**.

who → Personen   which → Dinge   that → Personen und Dinge

Bell was **the man who / that** invented the telephone.	Bell war der Mann, der das Telefon erfand.
He invented **machines which / that** changed the world.	Er erfand Geräte, die die Welt veränderten.

Willst du Zugehörigkeit oder Besitz ausdrücken, verwendest du bei Personen und Dingen **whose**.

That's the **boy whose** parents are doctors.	Das ist der Junge, dessen Eltern Ärzte sind.
Edinburgh is a **city whose** centre is very old.	Edinburgh ist eine Stadt, deren Zentrum sehr alt ist.

G7 Language tip: Das Gerundium

Gerund

Ein Gerundium bildet man, indem man **-ing** an ein Verb anhängt. Dadurch wird das Verb zu einem Nomen (Hauptwort). Mit dem Gerundium kann man über Tätigkeiten und Aktivitäten sprechen. Es steht am Satzanfang und ist **Subjekt / Satzgegenstand** des Satzes.

Watching TV can be interesting.	Fernsehen kann interessant sein.
Playing football is my favourite sport.	Fußballspielen ist mein Lieblingssport.

Das Gerundium kann aber auch nach dem Verb stehen und ist dann **Objekt / Satzergänzung** des Satzes. Das gilt besonders für Verben wie **love, (not) like** und **hate**.

I like **swimming**.	Ich schwimme gern.
I don't like **cleaning** my shoes.	Ich putze meine Schuhe nicht gerne.
Tim hates **tidying** his room.	Tim hasst es, sein Zimmer aufzuräumen.

Das Gerundium darf man nicht mit dem **present progressive** verwechseln. Vergleiche:

I **am** walk**ing** on the beach.	Ich gehe gerade am Strand spazieren.
I **love** walk**ing** on the beach.	Ich mag es, am Strand spazieren zu gehen.

G8 Die Zukunft mit will

Das Grammatikkapitel zur Zukunft mit will findest du im Orange Line 2 Workbook.

G9 Bedingungssätze Typ I

If-clauses type I

If-Sätze benutzt man, um Bedingungen und Folgen auszudrücken. Im if-Satz steht das **simple present**. Im Hauptsatz steht das **will-future**. Geht der **if**-Satz voran, steht am Ende des **if**-Satzes ein Komma.

Bedingung	Folge	
If it **rains**,	we'**ll stay** at home.	Wenn es regnet, bleiben wir zu Hause.
If it'**s** too dark,	I **won't take** any photos.	Wenn es zu dunkel ist, mache ich keine Fotos.

Im **if**-Satz steht nie **will / won't**!

Bedingungssätze können auch mit dem Hauptsatz beginnen. Dann entfällt das Komma.

I'**ll be** unhappy if you **don't come** to my party.	Ich werde unglücklich sein, wenn du nicht zu meiner Party kommst.

G10 Bedingungssätze Typ II

If-clauses type II

Bei Bedingungssätzen Typ II ist eine Bedingung unwahrscheinlich oder nicht erfüllbar. Du verwendest im if-Satz **simple past**. Im Hauptsatz steht **would / wouldn't + Grundform des Verbs**.

Bedingung	Folge	
If I **had** a dog,	I **would go** outside every day.	Wenn ich einen Hund hätte, würde ich jeden Tag nach draußen gehen.
If it **rained**,	I **would take** my umbrella.	Wenn es regnen würde, würde ich meinen Regenschirm mitnehmen.

Im if-Satz steht nie **would / wouldn't**.
Bedingungssätze können auch mit dem Hauptsatz beginnen. Dann entfällt das Komma.

I **would be** very sad if I **didn't find** my mobile again.	Ich wäre sehr traurig, wenn ich mein Handy nicht mehr finden würde.

Achtung Besonderheit: Statt **If I was** … wird oft **If I were** … gebraucht.

If I **were** you, I **would call** her.	Wenn ich du wäre, würde ich sie anrufen.

Im Deutschen verwendet man in beiden Satzteilen **würde**, **wäre** oder **hätte (Konjunktiv)**.

If your mum **didn't work** so hard, she **wouldn't be** so tired.	Wenn deine Mutter nicht so schwer arbeiten **würde**, **wäre** sie nicht so müde.

G11 Steigerung und Vergleiche von Adjektiven

Clauses of comparison

Adjektive mit **einer Silbe** steigerst du mit **-er / -est**:

cheap	cheap**er**	**the** cheap**est**	billig, billiger, am billigsten

Zweisilbige Adjektive, die auf **-y** enden, wie z. B. **happy**, **easy**, **crazy**, steigert man auch mit **-er / -est**.

happy	happ**ier**	**the** happ**iest**	glücklich, glücklicher, am glücklichsten

Alle anderen Adjektive **mit zwei und mehr Silben** steigerst du, indem du **more** und **the most** davor setzt.

expensive	**more** expensive **the most** expensive	teuer, teurer, am teuersten

Und so kannst du ausdrücken, dass etwas weniger oder am wenigsten ist:

interesting	**less** interesting **the least** interesting	interessant, weniger interessant, am wenigsten interessant

So kannst du Dinge miteinander vergleichen:

My big sister is **as** nice **as** my little brother.	Meine große Schwester ist genauso nett wie mein kleiner Bruder.
Mineral water is **not as** expensive **as** juice.	Mineralwasser ist nicht so teuer wie Saft.

Achtung: Um ungleiche Dinge zu vergleichen, benutzt du **than**.

London is **bigger than** Berlin.	London ist größer als Berlin.

G12 Some und any

Some and any

I need some milk but I don't need any cheese.

Ich brauche Milch, aber ich brauche keinen Käse.

Some oder **any** bedeuten im Deutschen **etwas**, **einige** oder **ein paar**.

In positiven Aussagen benutzt du **some**. Es muss nicht immer übersetzt werden.

I'd like **some** fruit.	Ich möchte gerne (etwas) Obst.
I must buy **some** carrots.	Ich muss (ein paar) Karotten kaufen.

In verneinten Aussagen und in den meisten Fragen steht **any**. Es wird nicht immer übersetzt.

Do you have **any** milk at home?	Hast du Milch zu Hause?
Sorry, we don't have **any** bread.	Es tut mir leid, wir haben kein Brot.

Wie **some** und **any** werden auch ihre Zusammensetzungen verwendet:

something und **anything**	(irgend)etwas
somebody und **anybody**	(irgend)jemand
someone und **anyone**	(irgend)jemand
somewhere und **anywhere**	irgendwo

He told me **something**.	Er hat mir etwas gesagt.
Did he tell you **anything**?	Hat er dir etwas gesagt?
No, he didn't tell me **anything**.	Nein, er hat mir nichts gesagt.

Achte auf folgende Übersetzungen:
not ... anything → nichts; not ... anybody / anyone → niemand; not ... anywhere → nirgendwo

G13 Gegenüberstellung: Simple present und present progressive

Simple present and present progressive

I usually don't drink juice, but today I'm drinking green juice because it's St Patrick's Day.

Normalerweise trinke ich keinen Saft, aber heute trinke ich grünen Saft, weil St. Patrick's Day ist.

Present progressive

Wenn du sagen möchtest, was gerade passiert oder was jemand im Augenblick tut, verwendest du das **present progressive**.

Signalwörter	
now	jetzt, nun
at the moment	im Moment

So bildest du Aussagen im **present progressive: am / are / is + Verb + -ing.**
So verneinst du die Sätze: **am / are / is not + Verb + -ing.**
Bei Fragen stellst du **am / are / is** an den Satzanfang.

Listen, your mobile **is ringing**.	Hör' mal, dein Handy klingelt gerade.
We **are not using** the computer at the moment.	Wir benutzen den Computer gerade nicht.
Are you **preparing** a snack?	Bereitest du gerade einen Imbiss vor?

Simple present

Wenn du einen Zustand beschreiben möchtest oder sagen willst, dass jemand etwas gewohnheitsmäßig tut oder dass etwas häufig oder regelmäßig geschieht, verwendest du das **simple present**.

He, **she**, **it** – das **s** muss mit!

Signalwörter	
every ...	jede / r / s
always	immer
usually	normalerweise
often	oft
sometimes	manchmal
never	nie

Mit **don't** oder **doesn't** (bei he, she, it) kannst du sagen, was man **nicht** macht.
Bei Fragen mit Vollverben (z. B. sing, write, play etc.) musst du **do** oder **does** verwenden.

Every year Keith celebrates St Patrick's Day.	Jedes Jahr feiert Keith den St. Patrick's Day.
Sue **doesn't** speak German.	Sue spricht kein Deutsch.
Do you often eat fish?	Isst du oft Fisch?

G14 Possessivpronomen

Possessive pronouns

I found a mobile. Is it yours?

Ich habe ein Handy gefunden. Ist es deins?

Du kennst bereits die Possessiv**begleiter** (**my**, **your**, **his**, **her**, **our**, **their**). Sie stehen **vor** einem Nomen. Mit den Possessiv**pronomen** kannst du sagen, wem etwas gehört, wenn **kein** Nomen **folgt**.

Possessive determiner	Possessivbegleiter	Possessive pronoun	Possessivpronomen
That's **my** umbrella.	Das ist **mein** Schirm.	It's **mine**.	Das ist **meiner**.
Is that **your** coat?	Ist das **deine** Jacke?	Is it **yours**?	Ist das **deine**?
This is **his** toothbrush.	Das ist **seine** Zahnbürste.	It's **his**.	Das ist **seine**.
This is **her** shampoo.	Das ist **ihr** Shampoo.	It's **hers**.	Es ist **ihrs**.
Look at the cat and **its** ball.	Schau dir die Katze und **ihren** Ball an.	It's **its**.	Das ist **ihrer**.
They are **our** bags.	Es sind **unsere** Taschen.	They are **ours**.	Es sind **unsere**.
Are they **your** towels?	Sind das **eure** Handtücher?	Are they **yours**?	Sind das **eure**?
This is **their** new car.	Das ist **ihr** neues Auto	It's **theirs**.	Das ist **ihrs**.

G15 Modale Hilfsverben

Modal auxiliaries

You mustn't walk.

Du darfst nicht gehen.

Modale Hilfsverben verändern die Art und Weise eines Verbs. **Can**, **can't**, **must**, **needn't**, **mustn't**, **may**, **may not** kommen immer zusammen mit einem anderen Verb vor.

I **can** play tennis.	Ich kann Tennis spielen. (Ich habe es gelernt.)
I **can't** play tennis now.	Ich kann jetzt nicht Tennis spielen. (Ich muss meine Hausaufgaben machen.)
You **must** play tennis with Amy.	Du musst mit Amy Tennis spielen.
He **needn't** play tennis.	Er braucht nicht Tennis (zu) spielen. (Wir sind genug Spieler.)
She **mustn't** play tennis.	Sie darf nicht Tennis spielen. (Sie ist krank.)
We **may** play tennis later.	Wir spielen vielleicht später Tennis. (Jetzt ist der Platz besetzt.)
They **may not** play tennis then.	Sie spielen dann vielleicht nicht Tennis. (Also können wir spielen.)

Aufgepasst bei **mustn't** (nicht dürfen) und **needn't** (nicht brauchen, nicht müssen):

You **mustn't** talk so loud.	Du darfst nicht so laut sprechen.
You **needn't** wait for me.	Du brauchst nicht auf mich (zu) warten. oder: Du musst nicht auf mich warten.

Audios zum Hörverstehen

Aufnahmeleitung: Ernst Klett Verlag
Redaktion: Lisa Poeira
Sprecherinnen und Sprecher: Brian Bowles, Harriet Carmichael, Annie Farr, Brian Fenton, Annemarie Gaillard, Grainne Gilles, John Hasler, Thomas Hunt, Helen Johns, Jamie McPhee, Rachael Miller, Claire Morgan, Richard Pearce, Nigel Pilkington, Suzy Riddell

Produktion: John Green, TEFL Audio, London
Tontechnik: Tim Woolf
Gesamtzeit: 23' 42"

Inhaltsverzeichnis der Audios zum Hörverstehen
Hörverstehenstexte aus dem Workbook

Zusätzlich:
- Alle Tracks des Workbooks als MP3-Dateien
- Lesetexte des Schülerbuchs als MP3-Dateien

Die Transkripte der Hörverstehenstexte aus dem Workbook finden Sie online auf www.klett.de unter **i8ce82.**

Weitere Übungsmöglichkeiten zu Orange Line 3:

Klassenarbeitstraining aktiv
978-3-12-548103-9

Vokabellernheft
978-3-12-548093-3

Grammatiktraining aktiv
978-3-12-548303-3

Vokabeltraining aktiv
978-3-12-548243-2

Vokabelübungssoftware
978-3-12-548643-0

Die Hörtexte gibt es auch online als MP3-Dateien zum Herunterladen. Dazu den Code **i8ce82** ins Suchfeld auf www.klett.de eingeben.